BOSTON PUBLIC LIBRARY
Copley Square

There Be
No
Dragons

WITHDRAWN

No longer the property of the
Boston Public Library.
Sale of this material benefits the Library.

From the Portuguese charts of the earliest voyages of discovery
in which terra incognita bore the legend,
"Beyond here there be Dragons."

There Be No Dragons

HOW TO CROSS A BIG OCEAN IN A SMALL SAILBOAT

Reese Palley

SHERIDAN HOUSE

To my years at sea . . . my only Past
To my wife, Marilyn . . . my loving Present
To my grandchildren . . . my unknowable Future

First published 1996 by
Sheridan House Inc.
145 Palisade Street
Dobbs Ferry, NY 10522

G525
.P335
1996

Copyright © 1996 by Reese Palley

All rights reserved. No part of this publication
may be reproduced, stored in a retrieval system
or transmitted in any form or by any means, electronic,
mechanical, photocopying, recording, or otherwise,
without the prior permission in writing of Sheridan House.

While all reasonable care has been taken in the publication
of this book, the publisher takes no responsibility for the use
of the methods or products described in the book.

Library of Congress Cataloging-in-Publication Data

Palley, Reese.
    There Be No Dragons: how to cross a big ocean in a small
sailboat/Reese Palley.
        p.   cm.
    ISBN 1-57409-010-0 (alk. paper)
    1. Voyages and travels. 2. Sailing. I. Title.
G525.P335 1996
910.4'5—dc20   96-41115
                                                        CIP

Editor: Janine Simon
Designer: Jeremiah B. Lighter

Printed in the United States of America

ISBN   1-57409-010-0

Contents

CONTENTS

INTRODUCTION

Anybody can cross a big ocean in a small boat. Books about ocean voyaging overromance dangers and overestimate required skills. This book will do neither. It is designed to address the basic problems, imagined and real, that keep sailors from the sea. It is designed to create a realistic framework of skills and attitudes into which any sailor, skilled or unskilled, experienced or tyro, young or ancient, man or woman, may realize the dream of passaging a big ocean in a small boat.

Modern materials and modern techniques have brought offshore passagemaking within the physical capabilities of any sailor. The basic need is for a reasonably seaworthy sailing vessel of 30 to 40 feet. Given the boat, the skills that are necessary for a safe offshore passage can be acquired by any sailor in less time than most of us spend in front of our TVs each year.

One day, about twenty years ago, I found myself toying with the outrageous conceit of sailing my own small boat across a big ocean. On that day I commenced a catalogue of the depths of my ignorance of the sea. This book was begun on that day. Had there been a book like this one available, I would have been able to see the shape of the tasks ahead of me. I would at least have had a friendly guide who would urge me on, as I do herein, and who would repeat the argument, which I iterate and reiterate, that you do not need to know everything about seamanship to sail over big oceans and that the only way to get ocean experience is to make an ocean passage. There was no such guide for me and I spent years floundering about in blind alleys that seemed to have no end. This book is just the guide that I would have wished for.

Fears of the sea, exacerbated in a hundred volumes dealing with the deep oceans, keep sailors tied to their moorings. This book argues that they are mostly myth and will further argue that the sailor is safer offshore in a blue water passage than in his own bathroom.

Sailing a big ocean is a perfectly legitimate dream. It is full of precedent. It is the beloved dream of Everyman and Everywoman. Ask them of their secret yearnings . . . they will answer, "The Sea."

It is a dream free of guilt, or should be. It is less a scheme to run away from care than a need to find a place and a time, away from our lemming world, where we may seek out and accept the natural responsibilities for our lives.

More dreams have been assassinated by guilt than ever were ended by waking up. The dream of freedom is a yearning towards growth, a need for self knowledge, not an escape from some half seen, half felt bogeyman. "Goodbye," the sailor's song says. "Goodbye to things that bore me. Life is waiting for me." That doesn't sound like escape to me.

We all have a need, mostly unsatisfied and rarely spoken, to measure ourselves against nature as we were meant to. To see how far our muscles and our breath and our unaided minds can take us. In a culture that lets us do little for ourselves we have this curious and hidden need to make our way to paradise on our own two feet. Being carried to paradise on a palanquin was, I am sure, as unsatisfying as being carried there on a jet. To sleep away your passage in silk draped sloth, or to murder space in a turbine's roar, gives us no measure of ourselves and the measure of self is the meaning of life.

On the great oceans of the world I found the opportunity to take measure of myself. Old, fat and unprepared, I did pretty good. So will you. Your dream is no different than mine. We all drink from the same cup, the trick is to find the well.

CHAPTER 1

The Sea and You

FIRST HURDLES

From dream to reality is the smallest of journeys, but when the line is crossed we find that the reality we confront is not always a pretty one. We might all share the same dream, but we cannot all share the same physical, let alone the same emotional capabilities.

When I crossed the line I was already over 50, overweight, and overdedicated to comfort. I was also overdrawn, overmortgaged, overlawyered, and overburdened by the loving cares of family. There was little that I could do about being over 50, but I was to learn later, a thousand miles at sea, that while the aging process does not exactly reverse itself in passagemaking, it does slow down; your peers left behind fatten and age as you shed pounds and years.

I am still sailing, much to the surprise of my progeny, 20 years and 35,000 miles later. On land you are planted and rooted. Movement of mind imitates the planting of body, and growth slows as age accelerates. At sea, afloat, all is movement, all is life. It all worked out very well for me.

Overweight is a piece of cake. There are no fat sailors and pounds magically melted as if wanded away at sea. Overly dedicated to comfort is more difficult. You must break the pattern of thought that says more comfort means a better life. The good life has damn-all to do with comfort. The good life has to do with stretching mind and body to their limits and beyond. If activity does not have outer parameters where hurt begins, then it is not enough. No pain, no gain.

We are all overdrawn and overmortgaged. The trick is to stop living in the future, where mortgages exist, and take the cash there is and live in the present, where sailboats and life exist. Overlawyered is easy. Get out to sea where the people who are seeking to get at you need a sailboat of their own to find you. If you can't be served you can't be sued.

Overburdened with family is the worst. Shedding family takes character. Those who love you will hooray you out to sea with joy and delight in your good fortune. Breaking out is a youthful decision, and when you do your kids will joyfully welcome you into their generation. A parent who rejects the life-diminishing burden of family guilt will be a parent who never demands guilt from the children. The folks to watch out for will not be your kids. They will be your contemporaries who will try to make you share their desperation. Do not allow it.

The reality of going to sea is a matter of casting aside all that negates your life, the vague imponderables that anchor you into some unknowable future. The passage to reality is littered with sailors stranded on the shoals of their expectations. It is difficult to wrench your world around to allow you freedom. And it is disastrous to have pie-in-the-sky expectations of what freedom will be like. The far shores of sailing are dotted with the abandoned boats and dreams of sailors who finally made it out there but found that all was not beam reaching and glorious sunsets. Sailing is hard, perhaps its chief attraction. On a long passage you either recast your expectations into something closer to the uncomfortable reality that you are experiencing or you will spend those weeks in disappointment, awaiting only the end of the passage to flee ashore.

Only in a small sailboat at sea are we reminded of our proper place in the universe. The sea forces upon us a natural scale. The sea limits one day's passage to a hundred miles, not too different from the scale used by the ancient Hebrews to measure the throne of God. The sea reminds us of the early modesties that made man great and refuses to allow its distances to be trammeled. Even a catamaran is too damn fast.

Small boat sailors parse the structures of the sea in days and weeks and months, not flashing minutes as the landbound do. They have recaptured nature's pendulum. The rhythms and stresses of the sea are the ancient imbedded memories of how our bodies want things to be. We sailors press more life into the years we are granted. And, because sailing is unstressing, we are granted more time in which to live. "Old sailors" is a cliche not without content.

On the earth we no longer have any subduing measure of greatness. Land has been smoothed for our wheels and the air above is furrowed by the flashing passage of our jets. It's just no fun anymore to journey about. We see ourselves coming even as we go, and we find ourselves waiting at both ends of our roamings.

Space and time . . . these gifts can best be savored from the deck of a cockleshell sailboat. A sailor's whole universe is only a circle with a three-mile radius, the distance his eyes can see to the horizon from sea level. It takes more than an hour of real time to sail from edge to edge of that tiny circle while, in the same sixty minutes, a jet ranges six hundred unfeeling miles. Passing through time and space in the sailor's small and personal world is the measure of natural coil . . . and we live better for it.

The first days offshore are terrible. They demand accommodation to seasickness and the hard regimens of a long sail. You will sleep badly those first nights, be tired and wet all the time, and you will feel certain that the rest of the passage and all future passages will be the same. By the third day, however, you will, if you allow yourself, gradually overcome the seasickness, learn how to keep dry, how to sleep and feed yourself, and how to conquer the small discomforts that prevent you from lifting your head to discover the glorious sunset that has been there all of the time. Some folk never allow themselves this transformation.

They fight it, cast their futures bleak, and hold tight to the discomforts they most decry. More pity to them.

If you want to go to sea you must have no expectations at all, neither of ill nor good, lest the foreboding of bad stuff should keep you ashore or lest the anticipation of wonderful stuff, which may be a bit delayed, should send you disappointedly home.

Leaving home is a little like dying. The longer and more distant the separation, the more fatal it feels. The changes involved in giving up life as you have known it for the unknowable adventures of the sea ahead of you are major and wrenching breaks, for you as well as for your family. You are giving up all of the hard-won and comforting support systems that cushion you. In a real sense, and possibly for the first time in your protected life, you are putting yourself out of reach of assistance, even in emergency situations. It is not easy either for you or for those you leave behind, and the parting must be accomplished, if not with total understanding on their part, then at least with their acceptance. When a sailor does actually take off for an unseen shore, a thousand miles away, it is no wonder that the folks left behind shake their heads in disbelief. How do you explain to family and friends that it is the opportunity to measure your own still unopened gifts that you seek? Those left behind are as bereaved as by a graveside. They are in agony over losing you as if the separation were real death. Their sense of loss can be so strong that it may diminish your resolve and bring self-doubt to your reasons for leaving. Tears of family are a solvent so powerful as to dilute your compelling need to live your life freely and fully. Where you see life, the family left behind sees only death.

No doting grandparents, lest they be passagemakers themselves, will easily understand or accept being parted from your kids should you haul your progeny with you. They see their own lives growing short and time becomes correspondingly precious. This is the mulch from which guilt grows. Sailor beware.

If you are taking your kids, be prepared for the unexpected. You might think that the prospect of great adventure on the high seas is irresistible, but they are more likely to be concerned with the terrible loss of precious friends and cousins. They will worry about school, about their social life, about being thought weird by the other kids, and a hundred childish matters no less real to them than your worries are to you. Kids are especially tender to change, to alterations of adolescent rhythms of such delicate balance, and so beset by youthful terrors, that perhaps neither logic nor lollipops will prevail.

But if they go with you their senses will reach out, flesh out as their bodies will, while not losing the smallest part of the wonder of childhood. Sailing kids mature more completely and at the same time more slowly. Their growth is paced and dignified, unpressured by the hothouse inputs of the faddy, competitive, and uncontrolled adolescent world they left behind.

At sea your kids will be the first to know the splendor of this gift. They will be the first to recognize the treasures of sense and sensibility that lie all about them, and the inexhaustible power that wells up in them from a knowledge of a responsible self and self-worth. Haul them along by the scruffs of their necks if that is the only way to get them to go. Their resistance will soon turn into gratitude and they will conjure up this souvenir long after other baubles you have offered them crumble to dust in memory and in reality.

When you make a passage you will learn that the seas are very large. Part of the charm of putting to sea, perhaps most of the charm, is the lack of clutter on the open waters. At sea you are sufficiently deprived of human sensory input so that, should events coalesce into the meeting of another passagemaker at sea, you will have gained the clarity to recognize, to savor, to appreciate, and to be thankful for the gift of another human spirit.

On land, companionship is thrust upon us, forcing us to be social long after we have had our fill of society. It is little wonder that we become cynics and come to hate our neighbors. And this is too bad, for beyond the companionship of our neighbors, and for some lucky few, the companionship of their God, we are quite alone in the universe. Only by seeking separation from the human herd can you become lovingly close to it. Just one more gift of paradox of which the sea is blessedly rich.

THE SEA AND YOU

Twenty-five years ago, when the Sir Francis Drake Channel in the British Virgin Islands was mostly empty, I found myself anchored off Peter Island. I was attracted ashore by some strange and wild music, reminiscent of Africa and Rio. It was coming from a large shack where the entire population of the island seemed to have gathered for a Saturday night dance.

The rhythms were black and infectious; the dancers were wild and transported. I wanted to jump in and lose myself among them. However, I felt so much an outsider that I hung out by the doorway and did not intrude with my white face into their private revels.

As I stood there, an old man danced by, older then than I am now, with a young girl in his arms upon whose breasts you could bounce a penny. He was drunk with the music and with his lady. His eyes missed none of my discomfort, none of my restraint, and none of my repressed desire to join in.

He danced around the room three times, each time closer. The last time, brushing my knees with his lady's backside, he leaned over her shoulder and said, "Give in, mon, give in, give in." He twirled his girl in front of me as if to show me the living I was missing and chanted again, "Give in, give in, give in, give in."

When later I went to the sea in earnest, I recalled the old man. His was the best advice I ever received about the sea and indeed about life itself. "Giving in" is about all that a small boat in a big ocean can do. As events and crises later overtook me, I learned that the sea can only be bested by giving in to her.

Accommodation to the sea is the only method of dealing with a force so vast that it will have its way no matter what you do. The very boat you sail is built on this principle. She accommodates herself to an overpowering wind by heeling in order to lessen the sail area. Her hull weighs nothing when afloat, and at speed offers no resistance of mass to its medium. When confronted by oncoming seas moving too quickly to handle, she slows down and reduces the probability of conflict. Just as it is impossible for a sailboat to exceed her hull speed, you must also realize that your capabilities, when compared to the forces of the sea you are conjuring, are chaff in the wind.

The prime survival principle at sea is accommodation. On board you "give in" to motions too quick to resist. You defeat seasickness only by accepting it. You accept that six knots is as fast as you will ever go. Although you might want your boat to move directly forward, you must always accept some lee and, although you might want to head toward 270°, you soon learn to gracefully compromise with the wind and steer for 230° or 310°. Knowing you cannot survive a hurricane, you compromise by not sailing where hurricanes are found. If you want to get somewhere in 30 days and the sea says 60, you accommodate yourself to her calendar and deep-six your own.

If you learn the lesson that you are a helpless mote in the great eye of the sea, if you come to accept her total hegemony over you, and if you offer servitude and subservience, you will suddenly and paradoxically find yourself in full charge of your life and your soul. When you learn that your mastery over the sea depends on your obedience, then you may go where and when you freely choose.

You may range the globe round and take ten years to do so. Should you not like the port you are in, there is always a better port over the horizon or, should you tire of the pressures of land altogether, you may, like Moitessier, choose to simply "go round again." You become free as no one on land can. But you must have care and remain humble, for although the world may become your oyster, your oyster still belongs to the sea.

FEAR AND TREPIDATION

Fear feeds on myth, and the vast and empty empire of the sea generates myth like a hull grows barnacles. These debilitating myths, fears of the known and the unknown, must be laid to rest before we can venture offshore. The eternal weapon against fear is the knowledge shared by others who have faced dangers, imagined and real, and survived. You must know how valid or invalid your fears of the sea are and take comfort from the knowledge that, for the few real dangers you will face, you have taken all reasonable precautions.

Here are the four categories of sea myths that, rationally or irrationally, paralyze us into remaining on land:

Things *not to be* afraid of because they do not exist.

Things *not to be* afraid of because they are exceedingly rare.

Things *not to be* afraid of because they can be dealt with.

Things *to be* afraid of (and how to think about them).

Things *Not to Be* Afraid of Because They Do Not Exist

MYSTERIOUS PLACES WHERE TERRIBLE THINGS HAPPEN

Mysterious tales of the Bermuda Triangle keep coming up like too much garlic in a Caesar salad. The cascade of creepy scenarios of the Triangle are as ingenious as they are false. To some it is the regular mischief that keeps the Devil from dying of boredom. Others paint images of great intergalactic space ships sucking up victims and vessels. Ship-devouring sea monsters are not as popular today as they were a hundred years ago, and only a few of us continue to believe that boats fall off the edge of a flat world. The truly inventive and the truly suspicious lay blame to our own government's experiments with diabolical weaponry.

I had a wonderful friend named Zelig who had a wonderful sailboat named *Callipygian* after his wife's behind. Callipygian means "lovely ass." Zelig was a blessed man, talented, handsome, brilliant, and a great surgeon who did not deserve the early death he suffered. He died alone on a ski slope a few minutes from a hospital where his life would have been saved. Like the rest of us, he would have preferred to go on his beautiful boat, beautiful wife at hand, and his hand on the tiller. This was not to be. Nor was the similar, early, and unnecessary death of *Callipygian* which started as a mystery and ended as a cautionary tale.

Callipygian was in Bermuda, at one angle of the Bermuda Triangle, and Zelig, a busy surgeon, was unable to find the window of time to bring her home. He found a skipper with a seemingly adequate history of sailing and many references from previous owners. The contract to bring *Callipygian* home was signed and the passage was commenced on a mild and sunny afternoon in June. The hired skipper, a bit long in the tooth and a bit wider in the girth, anticipated a milk run and sought out as crew two unseasoned nubiles whose talents ran to presenting curves rather than handling lines. But Bermuda to New York seemed less of a challenge for this no longer young skipper than was the prospect of "passaging" with girls.

Just as he crossed the axis of the Gulf Stream, a nice little wind, neither gale nor terrifically fierce, came down out of the cold north and commenced to heap up seas. Still trying to make his schedule, the skipper opted to beat into seas and wind. The girls, his only crew, were terrified. Early in the storm one fell and hurt her back and the other cowered below with seasickness and terror. Rather than turn tail and wait out the blow, the skipper panicked and, in a perfectly sound boat, sent an SOS for assistance.

A nearby freighter plucked them off *Callipygian* which they abandoned with an open companionway hatch. She quickly disappeared in the midst of the storm and the skipper later testi-fied that she was a "doomed vessel" and that from the deck of the rescuing freighter he watched her sink. A year later, *Callipy-gian*, crewless, her companionway hatch wide open to the sea, was sighted bobbing about in the North Atlantic a thousand miles from the U.S. coast. Two years later, still crewless, she was again sighted, this time with somewhat less of a bob and lower in the water, two thousand miles from our shores. She was never heard from again.

The real explanations of disappearances in the Triangle are considerably less exotic and less likely to be splashed about in the sensation-seeking press. It is a matter of mathematics, aided by geography, and abetted by bubble-headed skippers. On the edge of the open sea, between Cape Hatteras and Florida, there are more pleasure boats per square mile than anywhere else in the world. The immutable laws of chance dictate that the more boats in a given area, the higher the probability of disaster.

Nowhere in the world are there more unprepared and un-trained dimwits sailing about in the open sea. Few know how quickly the sea can ferret out any lack of seamanship in an emer-gency. The skippers' lack of capability is reinforced by the inad-equacies of the boats they operate. Boats are built in a climate of fierce cost and price slashing, in which a responsible boatbuilder can be buried under a flood of Clorox bottles. Sooner or later these lightly stuck together cockleshells find themselves round-ing Hatteras in a norther and in trouble. As the warm Gulf Stream churns north and east to escape the jut of Cape Hatteras, it runs smack into the cold weather patterns out of the North At-lantic. Hot and cold air explosively mix together immediately off the Cape, the favored route of pleasure boats. When the wind roars down from the north against the flow of the Stream, it heaps up destructive and dangerous seas over these shallow wa-ters. When untrained and physically limited crew in inade-quately built boats find themselves in the occasional maelstrom of the Stream, some are not going to make it.

All of the reasons cited above explain why so many boats come-a-cropper in the Triangle. The "mysterious disappearance" freaks conspiratorially ask, "Why here, and only here, do so many boats in trouble for whatever reason simply disappear? They do not in other difficult areas . . . so why here?"

The answer is simple geography. In the Triangle there is no close downwind shore or jumble of islands upon which an unlucky (lucky?) sailor can be cast by prevailing winds from the west. Eastward of the Triangle there is no land for three thousand miles. A boat in trouble is very likely to remain unsighted as it sinks far offshore in the empty stretches of the Atlantic into which it has been carried by the prevailing easterlies. Disappearance "without a trace" is no surprise in these waters.

SEA MONSTERS

The only sea monsters (and dragons) left are those that inarticulately jerk about in Japanese horror films. Not much real danger here.

LOSING ONE'S WAY AT SEA

Put me anywhere, in any ocean in the world, without radio or electronics, without sextant, watch, or compass, with the sun obscured by day and the stars and moon obscured by night, and I will find my way to land within 30 days. It is impossible not to find land *somewhere*. I may have a hairy moment locating a safe port after making a landfall, but I can always wait about after sighting land, till some convenient fisherman comes along to help me on my way, or the contrail of a jetliner points to an airport, or the smell of urban sewerage invites me to simply follow my nose, or even the welcoming loom of a city.

Forget about getting lost. If you have no navigational instruments you need only follow the prevailing winds either toward or away from the rising sun (doesn't matter which) and, unless you are below 60° South Latitude (I cannot imagine why you would be), land will rise up over your bow in less than a month. As the guy who sells parachutes says, "You have my money-back guarantee."

Things *Not to Be* Afraid of Because They Are Exceedingly Rare

THE WHALE

There is one peril against which there is simply no defense. That is the whale. But lest you let this one-and-only unhandleable hazard keep you ashore, let me add that of the thousands of sea passages of the last 50 years, I know of only a handful of boats which were attacked by a whale. Even in these cases the liferafts saved most of the lives.

PIRACY

Piracy does not happen very often but when it does it is at your invitation. Pirates (this terrible name almost does not apply anymore) are generally timid and terrified third-world fishermen who make an attempt on a yacht only if certain there will be no resistance. Demonstrate your alertness and your will to fight off an attack, and successful piracy will never occur even in the worst waters around the South China Sea. Avoid obviously bad neighborhoods as you would sensibly avoid troublesome streets at home. There are only a few places in the world where piracy continues to be a problem: the Strait of Malacca, the Philippines, Malaysia, in and around Panama and the Suez Canal, and in any marine chandler shop.

The image of pirates armed to the teeth with automatic weapons and high-speed chase boats is the stuff of Hollywood, not of the real sea. Our modern pirate is seldom more than a poor man with a machete in a homemade wooden boat. Turn a bright light on him and he will dissolve into the darkness, dissuaded of evil intent. For the hard cases, carry a shotgun and let off a few rounds in the air if you sense the presence of a suspicious fishing boat. That is usually all the defense needed.

Things *Not to Be* Afraid of Because They Can Be Dealt With

SEASICKNESS

The fear that keeps more people off the sea and away from their heart's desire is the fear of getting seasick. Granted that this is the worst of feelings, and that in the throes of it you fear life more than death, and would rather be done with it. Granted that it is undignified and messy and incapacitating. Granted all these things, it will pass only if you give it a chance. Seasickness rarely lasts more than three days. The problem is that most folk get their first experience of the sea during an afternoon sail. Sure they get sick. We all do. But after the third day, even without medication, the world brightens as the *sea change* takes place.

Everyone gets seasick at some point. It is neither a disgrace to be sick nor an honor if you are not. It comes with the territory and is bearable if it is accepted as part payment for the pleasures of the sea. It is no longer even necessary to bear this curse. Adhesive patches that leach scopolamine through the skin in molecular doses are effective, and are absent of most unpleasant side effects. Just knowing that relief is available makes the *mal* of the *mer* less likely to keep you from exotic ports and South Pacific sunsets.

The real cure for seasickness is the sea change itself, and it is the sea change that will become the ultimate reason you continue to go to sea. It is that moment, a few days into the passage, when seasickness, aches from boat bites, chafe, and ennui all disappear and you are reborn into a world of wonder. A world that smells, looks, feels, and sounds different—and better—than anything you have ever known.

BOREDOM

"But what do you do with all your time? Aren't you bored?" I have heard that question so often that, at times, I begin to wonder if maybe I do get bored at sea and simply do not recognize it. But I really know better. The paradox is that the small spaces of a sailboat, shorn of outside influence, become a vast playground for the endless investigation of the most fascinating subject of self. With such rich material who could really be bored? To have the rare and wonderful privilege of spending 30 days or so finding out just who I really am does not impress me as a hardship. In fact, we would all be better off were we each sentenced to a month of introspective aloneness at the top of a mountain, or on a passage between Galápagos and Tahiti.

Real boredom is reading the damn newspapers with their stories of violence and deceit. Boredom is viewing the broadcast recasts of faked feelings and unreal emotions. Boredom is dealing each day with your family soap opera, when tension becomes the false analog of life. Boredom comes from watching life, not from participating in it. At sea there are no spectators. At sea you are the ultimate participant.

LONELINESS

Our world is only peopled by what is inside our own heads. When Slocum found himself in need of a companion he conjured up Columbus. When I feel the need for discourse I riff through the list of minds that I have enjoyed. They are all aboard with me, in my head or in my library, waiting patiently to keep me company.

And I never sail solo. I always sail with a companion with whom I have the glorious opportunity to unhurriedly explore a relationship. Sometimes I learn something of my companion. All the time I learn something of myself. There is no loneliness at sea. Only *aloneness* and that is quite a different thing.

ILLNESS

If you are an old guy with a history of heart problems then you must measure the known risk against the known rewards of an ocean passage. If you have an over-ripe appendix have it out.

It is surprising that, of the entire depressing litany of illnesses of the flesh that bedevil us, there are serious consequences to the sailor in only an unanticipated *young* heart attack and an unanticipated appendicitis. The game is well worth the candle, and the fear of illness, when looked at coolly, is mostly exaggerated. With very small differences, illnesses that will kill you at sea will just as surely turn you toes-up on land.

ACCIDENTS

I do not need actuarial charts to convince myself that I am safer from accidents at sea than I am on land. The number of things that can damage you on a small vessel on an ocean passage are demonstrably fewer than the carnage that awaits you in your own hometown. The most dangerous place in the world is your automobile within a mile of the house you live in. The second most dangerous place, according to those who claim to know, is your own bathtub.

It is possible to have a serious accident at sea but you would have to work at it. Only a wildly swinging boom can fatally hurt you and it is much more in your power to prevent an uncontrolled jibe than it is to stay out of the way of the drunk behind a hundred horses intent on your maceration. You get thrown about a lot, sometimes savagely, on a small boat, but, because the boat design limits your motion, the results are usually little more than bad bruises.

Things *to Be* Afraid of (and How to Think about Them)

STORMS

We are all terrified of storms until we weather our first gale. Then we discover that our boat and our selves are good at surviving storms, indeed are built to survive storms, and much of the terror disappears. Gales are so infrequent that sailors rarely experience a dangerous one in a lifetime of sailing. In January, the percentage probability of gales in the North Atlantic is only ten percent. Few of us are likely to go seeking them during this vicious month. In June the Atlantic is a pussycat. By combining caution with nature's blessed infrequency, you can easily arrange to avoid any sustained breeze much over 25 knots.

Certainly a sailor must be prepared for storms. Certainly you and your boat must be so contrived that both will survive anything but for a storm in which you should not be caught in the first place. But to allow a fear of storms, rare as they are, to keep you from the sea is a bad bargain. Look to the preparation of your vessel and look to your pilot charts. It is much more likely that a safe will drop on your head in your hometown than you, exercising a modicum of caution and common sense, will meet an ultimate, or even penultimate, storm in the deep oceans.

Be warned that the preceding remarks refer to the deep oceans. Longshore even a small wind can quickly bash you on the rocks. Carefully choose your time of approach to land. If things do not smell just right as you near your destination, heave to, put your feet up, have a bottle of beer, and wait till the odors of land improve.

HURRICANES AND TYPHOONS

There is no reasonable excuse for getting caught in one of these ultimate storms. There are plenty of places and times in the oceans of the world in which these monsters are totally and predictably absent. Sailing during cyclonic seasons is simply not part of offshore passaging. If you choose to do so, at least do not subject your innocent crew to your suicidal tendencies. To those of you more sensible and more in love with life (why else would you be contemplating an ocean passage?), read the pilot charts and leave cyclones to the fools.

BEING RUN DOWN BY A BIG SHIP

If a proper watch is mounted it is almost impossible to have a collision. During both daytime and nighttime you have at least 15 minutes, and sometimes as much as one hour, to determine the course and the speed of a sighted vessel. In that time you can easily set up a course that guarantees you will clear each other. In most encounters a big ship's bridge will be aware of you long before you are aware of it. If not, you have plenty of time to signal your presence with lights or by radio. Sailors who get killed in collisions are only those who play a seagoing Russian roulette by substituting an hour of sleep for a careful watch.

These are the sea myths, the entire collection of confrontations that either do not exist, are wildly exaggerated, or can be easily dealt with.

There are few dangers at sea, only problems to be solved. If you ignore the obvious solutions then you have a right to be fearful. But if you take the most basic care of yourself and your boat, you will bury your fears where they belong, deep in a thousand fathoms. Let not fear of fear keep you from the sea.

DEPENDENCE AND INDEPENDENCE

Most sailing in the U.S. is *in utero*, firmly attached by umbilical cords to marina and boatyard and shops, cords that stretch back from the boats to a thousand harbors along the coast. Rather than a source of strength, these ties to land serve more to deny freedom than to satisfy need. These umbilical cords are limiting of range and activity, the two elements that most define the offshore passagemaker.

The basic difference between offshore and umbilical-cord sailing is attitudinal. One attitude assumes that the sailor must be at the receiving end of a long and expensive cornucopia that, at the twitch of desire, satisfies all needs, both real and imagined. This ease of material satisfaction, this attitude toward attachment, denies the umbilical sailor the delight of horizons too far for the cords to stretch.

For the offshore sailor, "I am what I am" translates into "I have what I have." Shed of all of those acquired and imposed needs for equipment and supplies so efficiently foisted upon us by a creative marine industry, it can be demonstrated that to sail offshore you need have only "what you have." I have known passagemakers with so little equipment, and that which they did have so unsophisticated, that I could not decide whether to stand in disdain of their carelessness or stand in awe of their courage. In order to cross great oceans one needs little more than a way to keep the ocean out. Experienced sailors, as well as many with little experience, have done this and continue to do just that.

The multiple overlays of modern equipment are more quilts of comfort than bedrocks of necessity. Those who sleep on a deck and cover themselves with the stars need neither to air the mattress nor do laundry. Comfort or freedom, the ultimate choice for modernity, goes far beyond the question of where we sail. The trading away of freedom in exchange for ease is just more clearly seen, as are most things, when sailors face themselves on the open sea.

If we commence with the attitude that comfort is more important than freedom we will never get to sea. Comfort builds prison ships of convenience that, entangled by dock lines, water hoses, and great hanks of yellow electrical cords, will not float, let alone go to windward. Once this habit of dependence, the other side of the coin of inadequacy, is established, it is almost impossible to break.

The need for equipment is reinforced by the strange mindset of many Americans who firmly believe that hobbies must be accessorized to be rewarding. It is a simpleminded belief, enthusiastically peddled by the sports industries, that equipment makes the sport and that the better the equipment, the more the equipment, and the more expensive the equipment, the better the sport. This is demonstrable fiction. Sailing on a board and holding a stick for a mast requires more skill and provides more sport than anything needing more complicated equipment. Taking an unaccessorized boat as a starting point, the same view holds. The more you burden a boat with equipment beyond what is absolutely the required minimum, the shorter is your range and the less your fun. Unnecessary stuff weighs down your boat and burdens you with the need to serve machines that, in lesser quantities, would better be serving you.

I will not argue here for naked and reckless exposure to the open oceans. I believe in taking whatever small advantage that you can over the intimidating power of the sea. I will argue that almost all of the advantages gained from equipment lie on a margin that decreases exponentially with increases in the cost of equipment. You must not be kept from the sea and from your heart's desire by the fear that you cannot go out there without a radar, a GPS, a diesel generator, and a foulweather suit of which you would need three spare sets.

The attitude that the gear is the sport or that the media is the message must be broken. Once this umbilical cord is cut, the startling discovery is made that, given an irrepressible craving for freedom, we can do with damn-all. We discover at sea that, when the occasion arises, we are perfectly capable of repairing the small amount of equipment that we really need with the simplest tools.

MINIMUMS

How do you determine what you really need? How do you cry "enough!" to a seemingly endless process of acquiring objects and information that might well be keeping you on land?

Almost all equipment and most knowledge is superfluous for sailing across an ocean. The level of sophistication and expenditure will depend only upon the limitation of your pocketbook. Going offshore involves a "means test," the basic assumption of which is, "Any expenditure that keeps you from the sea need not be made." If the cost of equipment is the price of freedom, then do without.

Very much the same problem arises in the matter of knowledge and information, but the problem is usually time, not money. There is no end to the things that can be learned prior to an offshore passage. Should this endless process prevent your departure, then you must declare not only "I have what I have" but one further variation, "I know what I know and what I know is sufficient."

The real transfer of knowledge of the sea, of how to sail on the sea, takes place at sea and from the sea directly to you. There are few times at sea when you need answers for your survival that cannot be found within the physical evidence of the moment. You can listen to lectures and study book illustrations for months and yet learn only half of what your first night watch at sea will teach about the importance, for example, of big ship navigation lights.

The more you know, the safer and the more comfortable the passage. But to know evermore before you go to sea you must expend evermore time. In the expenditure of time, as with the expenditure of money, the marginal increment of advantage at sea for more time spent in study on land decreases sharply after the initial and surprisingly small portion of important stuff is tucked away under your hat. In preparing yourself for the sea you must always measure the time that is being traded—not only how much you are adding to your knowledge.

What is vital is a matter of judgment and perspective, a matter of trading material and informational impediment for the rare and wonderful chance to take a shot at the sea yourself. All you need is to survive the first passage. You need not survive it elegantly or comfortably, just survive it. If your first passage is too comfortable and does not challenge your knowledge, then you have waited too long. You have wasted time at sea, which is wasting life itself.

The Absolute Minimum Knowledge

These are only six subjects which the skipper newly bound off-shore must master to make safe passages.

THE THREE D'S OF MARINE CHARTS

The three D's are the ability to read the charts for Depth, Distance, and Danger. The ability to be instantly aware that *depth* is changing is as crucial as is the ability to translate the *distance* scale of the chart into a working reality of what actually lies over the bow.

Navigational *dangers* are usually associated with navigational aids. The presence of any aid to navigation should signal the sailor that trouble is brewing ahead. Navlights must be read, their periodicity understood, and you must be able to predict *from the chart* where and when they will appear.

To accomplish this the skipper will need to recognize the chart icons that carry so much information. You must be aware that every bit of information on a chart is crucial. You should understand the chart correction process and the numbering and dating systems of the charts in use.

When you are far offshore, marine charts are useless. The real importance of charts, and of the information they carry, only becomes evident as the sailor approaches land. The most crucial charts are those that aid in entering unfamiliar harbors.

It is most important to recognize and perceive the static, artificial, two dimensionality of charts as compared with the three-dimensional and ever-changing view of the real world over your bow. This ability to extrapolate reality from the printed shorthand of charts is a learned response that comes to the sailor only through practice and experience at sea. First you must know what the little marks on the charts mean. Then, only with experience of the sea itself, your mind will transpose this shorthand into the geographic reality that spreads out before you. The first time you successfully enter an unfamiliar harbor will be the true beginning of your education. This process cannot happen in the classroom. It can only happen at sea. Ultimately the sea is the only teacher.

HOW TO READ LIGHTS AND TRACK TRAFFIC

The safest way to sail is to be in chronic terror of every ship that looms up over the horizon. Every ship that appears in your sailing circle, day or night, represents a potential for collision. Collisions are rare and easily avoided, but the skipper must be capable and willing, in both darkness and daylight, to track every ship and every light that appears.

Tracking, not identification, is the overriding justification for the existence of ship lights. They are designed so that little knowledge or experience is needed to determine the direction, angle, and speed of a ship sighted at night. While the theory can be acquired in a Power Squadron course or from a book, you must stand at your helm and come to understand, in the very moment of the event, just what unfolds as you track a light from its first tentative bob over the horizon till it eases safely outside of your sailing circle. Height, separation, color, and speed of navigational lights all define the track of a ship that passes in the night. If the lights can be read the vessel can be tracked. If the vessel can be tracked both vessels are safe.

HOW TO READ A COMPASS

The offshore sailor must be familiar with compass deviation and variation and must be able to convert the hard, true directions printed on the chart to the soft magnetic directions observed on the compass. You must understand the limitations as well as the precious advantages of your magnetic compass. Your compass must be as familiar as the back of your hand.

HOW TO HAND, REEF, AND STEER

Sail handling on long passages is a gross art, not a fine one, and only the barest minimum of experience in sail trim is needed. Handing sail, putting them up and taking them down under difficult conditions, is a learned skill about which little can be known save in the doing at sea. The sailor quickly gets the feel of sail handing from actual events. It is a skill learned by your muscles not by your mind. Handing sail must never be done quickly. Slow and steady is the way to go.

I read a dozen books on the techniques of reefing before I ever was faced with the pressing need to reduce sail at sea. I learned more in the first ten minutes of rising wind in a light gale than from all of the books put together. Learn the basic procedures for a jiffy-reef from any scruffy dockside lounger. You will discover that all you need to know is which line to haul and in what order. What is crucial at sea is not so much a vast experience in reefing but the urgent compulsion to recognize that the moment for shortening sail is approaching. Nothing is truer than the observation that when you start thinking about reefing it is too late. Incidentally, if you do not have jiffy-reefing installed on your boat, get it.

Steering, like reefing, is also acquired in the doing. Steering is much like learning to ride a bicycle, first it looks impossible and then, once learned, it is never forgotten. Most boats are sufficiently forgiving that it is difficult to make a really serious steering error in a big ocean. You have all that room to correct your error. If you know enough to avoid a jibe all standing, then you know enough about steering to go to sea.

HOW TO USE A SIMPLE RDF

A simple radio direction finder will always get you to harbor safely and without too much confusion. An RDF is a close-in instrument. As you close land, it will unerringly tell you what precise position you are closing (from the Morse-coded RDF beacons), and the closer you get the more accurate will be its ability to lead you there. You should first practice with it upon entering your own harbor. Reading an RDF is like developing a relationship with a lover. You will get lots of mixed signals, but, if you persevere, you are likely to end up both happy with your mate and safe in harbor.

Alas, as it is with human relationships, RDF is a tricky business, full of potential for error and misdirection. If you come to know where the errors will appear, and if you learn to listen to and trust the dots and the dashes, RDF can become for you what is has become for me, my preferred electronic navigational aid. The real nice thing about RDF, especially the cheap handheld models, is that they are about as high-tech as your doorbell. They always work.

HOW TO TAKE A NOON SIGHT

Absolutely a piece of cake. All you need is an eye (two is a luxury), a cheap sextant, and a math table. The math is addition and subtraction and you do not even need to know the time of, nor indeed anything about GMT. The only problem with a noon sight is that you can only take it at noon. If clouds are around when noon comes around, you must wait until the next day. Oh well, at sea you have little else to do anyway.

That's it. That is all you need to know. That is *absolutely* all you need to know. With these simply learned skills, you are safer crossing to Bermuda or Hawaii than you are crossing Long Island Sound.

The Absolute Minimum Equipment

You need only eleven pieces of cheap equipment for an offshore passage.

You could, of course add a thousand other things to my list. If you do, you might increase your chances of completing the crossing a mite, but not by much.

A binnacle and hand-bearing compass

The pilot chart for the month of your passage

The harbor chart for your destination, and alternate charts should you be blown off-course

A plastic sextant

The table of declinations of the sun

A quartz timepiece and stopwatch

A medical chest

A handheld RDF

A GPS

In addition you will need two relatively expensive items. Consider borrowing or renting them.

A liferaft

An EPIRB (Emergency Position Indicating Radio Beacon)

Your boat is your major prior expense but I assume that you already own a boat and that you are "going with what you got." Thirty feet is plenty, 25 is possible and 40 is best. Anything bigger will usually require more crew, more gadgetry, and lots more money.

Concerning the needed knowledge, think about those skills you already possess. You can read a chart. You know that red is port and green is starboard, and that of the two white lights on a distant big boat the shorter one is always forward. You can read a compass. You have some little experience in handing, reefing, and steering, and if you do not yet know how to shoot the sun for latitude at noon, any sailor can show you how in ten minutes.

In all probability and as unlikely as it seems, you are already sufficiently equipped and sufficiently knowledgeable to skipper your boat over a big ocean. Honest.

REGAINING CONTROL

We Americans have a noble, if dated and unworkable, image in our immediate past of how the human animal should live. The Crees and Apaches and Navajos made a better bargain than we have or ever will. They lived close to the land. The sun, the moon, the winds, and the seasons established the rhythms of their lives. They gathered and hunted and prepared the stuff they needed for life. When life became burdensome they took themselves to the top of the mountain, close to the Great Spirit, and allowed themselves to be gathered in. Certainly too romantic and unattainable a reality in our world, but the image remains as attractive as it is improbable. Much as we yearn for freedom we are enslaved to sloth and service. There is no emancipation on land.

Convenience creeps up on us, surreptitiously chipping away at our ability and our inclination to do for ourselves. We are being robbed of a significant part of our lives, the part allowing us to control the small decisions and actions that eventually form the quality of our lives.

When we no longer are allowed to fetch and carry, to produce directly the things that we eat and use, to repair with our own hands the devices that surround us, then we are reduced from a whole being to the least important fraction, the consuming fraction, of what we are capable.

The real problem is not the ubiquitous convenience that is offered us on land. The real problem is that we are human and corruptible and are unable to avoid forming habits that first feel good but then quickly lead to addiction. We make a Faustian bargain, trading away the control of self and receiving in return habits of sloth that diminish our bodies and our minds. Within the landlubberly parameters of oversupply, permissiveness, and convenience, there exists no natural mechanisms that might first allow us to resist and then to cast off self-destructive patterns of living.

The sea is the last hope we have for accepting responsibility for our own lives and the easy opportunity for our own deaths. Only at sea lies emancipation. Only at sea do we regain the free choice of life or death. Only at sea can the end of life come so naturally, *sans* tubes, *sans* hospitals, *sans* lugubrious doctors and, most of all, *sans* guilty children.

CHAPTER 2

Getting Ready

The final test for every proposition discussed in this book is:

> Does the proposition address a fear of the sea that keeps sailors ashore?
>
> Is the proposition couched in simple enough terms for the newest sailor among us?

The sole purpose of this chapter is to get you ready to sail a big ocean in a small sailboat. To do so fears and anxieties that relate to preparation must be laid to rest in the simplest possible terms. While this chapter is hardly exhaustive, it is sufficient. Sufficient is the watchword. Sufficient for a beginner. Sufficient to get you off your duff and aboard.

THE TECHNICAL LITERATURE OF THE SEA

Most preparation for going to sea happens only after you are at sea. It is on-the-job training and that makes the cautious among us apprehensive (what sailor should not be?). We can never know what it really feels like to read a chart at sea until we are at sea . . . but we can know what charts to read and what they mean. Surprisingly few sailors know what is available to them in the literature of the sea, of which charts are only one part.

What follows is a ramble through this literature, an investigation not only of what is available but how each publication functions and how it should be used. This is the true beginning of any ocean passage.

The printed resources available to the offshore sailor are immense. They cover all the eventualities that other sailors have overcome and have become a compendium of all knowledge about the seas over which you wish to sail.

Although I believe that sailing schools have little to offer to those of us who want to go offshore, I do believe that all beginning sailors, and even some old hands, would benefit by a disciplined curriculum covering all of the vast panoply of printed material that is readily and cheaply supplied by the U.S. government. This section will identify, explain, and comment on all tracts and chartings pertinent to going offshore in a small vessel. I have tried to be succinct but, by the nature of the material, the presentation can be turgid. Persevere. The more dense it seems here the more clear will be your vision out there.

You should commence your passagemaking long before you put to sea. Passage of the mind and spirit can be sailed safely in a small room in your own home. We shall call it your Chart Room.

Creating A Chart Room

You start with The Defense Mapping Agency. Almost everything that you will need will be available from this agency or from others closely related. The Defense Mapping Agency offers nautical charts and publications in nine individual catalogs, each covering a different region of the world. Each catalog contains general, ordering, and nautical products information, lists of charts, and a listing of chart sales agents. The catalogs are free of charge and available from your local NOAA chart sales agent or may be ordered from the NOAA Distribution Branch.

CHART IDENTIFICATION

"Chart Numbering System." This system will enable you to know in advance the level of detail of a chart and its geographical location and the kind of information that it contains without ever having seen it.

CHART TERMS AND SCALE

Here you learn the perverse fact that "a large area chart is called small scale" and one covering a small area "is called large scale." Memorize it. Do not try to derive the logic.

In *Charts Under Red Lights*, there is a discussion very much the concern of a small boat sailor. At night at sea, when you are trying to preserve your night vision, you will constantly pop below to check this light or that buoy. You will use a red light to do it but the suggestion to "highlight" your chart ahead of time is wise.

Safety at sea for the small boat sailor is not often a matter of large considerations. It often comes down to how to read a chart when it is raining, your glasses are fogged, and to preserve your vision you can only allow yourself the dimmest of red lights. It doesn't sound important perhaps, but just wait until you are out there.

WORLD CHARTS

They cover large areas so they are small scale charts. To paste the world on your chart room walls with these you would need 36 charts that cannot be directly related and overlaid because their scales are all different. There is an easier and cheaper set of charts.

These are the "World International Charts." All numbered below 100, they include the entire world in only fourteen charts. They are *all* the same small scale of 1:10,000,000. They will all neatly match up and if your wall is big enough, you will have a wonderful array of charts on which to plot the voyages of all the legendary sailors you read about and, eventually, to plot your own first, tentative essays into imaginary passages. Even those legendary sailors began in this way. You are already well along in becoming a legend of your own.

CHART SYMBOLS AND ABBREVIATIONS

This is a list of all of the mysterious little symbols and the even more mysterious abbreviations that you will need to understand as you read nautical charts. You cannot read a chart without it. A first and absolute must. Symbols and abbreviations are the true language of the passaging sailor. Should you not get all this tucked neatly under your belt before your passage, at some point, as sure as little fishes, your ignorance will lead you into trouble.

INTERNATIONAL FLAGS AND PENNANTS

There is a language peculiar to the sea. Since the advent of radio ship-to-ship communication there is less and less need to know your flags. But flags are an ancient and integral part of the lore of the sea and putting all of that romance aside will detract from your pleasure of communication.

We once entered English Harbour on Antigua after a transatlantic passage during which we lost all mechanical and electrical power. We entered under sail; those of you who know that busy place will appreciate our terror that we might do damage. Without any other means of communication we, perhaps with not too much conviction, ran up the two signal flags that carry the message, "Beware, we are navigating without power." The message was lost on most folk at anchor but one, saltier than the rest, read and broadcast it via VHF to the other boats at anchor. Five minutes after the flags went up, we were surrounded by dinghies offering assistance. The most appreciated was the sailor who came laden with bread and fresh fruit.

The section on Morse symbols will help not only with radio but with Navlights and beacons as well.

SMALL SCALE WORLD CHARTS

Small scale world charts are three, six-foot long charts of the world that can easily substitute for the 14 World International Charts. Ultimately the Chart of the World is an almost five-feet long, single sheet chart of the world.

PILOT CHARTS

Pilot charts are the key to all ocean passages. If you can have only one chart on any voyage it would have to be the pilot chart.

PLOTTING SHEETS

These are blank sheets onto which, with a little skill, you can transfer any chart, magnify to any scale any area for which you have a chart, and create ocean charts to track a passage for which there may be no applicable charts at all. This ability to "roll your own" is invaluable.

SAILING DIRECTIONS AND GUIDES

PACIFIC ISLANDS

One of the classic coastal pilots of which there is one for every coast in the world. *The Pacific Island Pilot* is special. Who among us has not dreamed of these places and passages. This volume will give you the taste of enroute sailing directions. Get to know it carefully. Dig into all the categories of information it hides. Make a chart of Papeete Harbor. Who knows, you may need it.

NORTH ATLANTIC OCEAN (Planning Guide)

The planning guides are a breed apart. Unlike coastal pilots that concentrate on longshore, planning guides are heavy on deep ocean information such as weather and waves, visibility and temperatures, and much more. You should always make your passage with the planning guides. In the absence of charts, planning guides will get you to the area of your landfall and the enroutes, also in the absence of charts, will help you make your landfall.

Books, Manuals And Catalogs

AMERICAN PRACTICAL NAVIGATOR

Whatever it is that you need to know concerning seamanship is contained herein. It is not easy reading but it is not meant to be. Almost every facet of an offshore passage that is dealt with in this book can be sourced in the APN. There are two volumes and you will need both. You will need them first for your chart room and then on board your vessel to help you through the bad spots. What is a bobbing light? How do you measure distance off? What are the values for the Beaufort Scale? How does the surface of the sea look in each of these values? The questions and the answers roll on like the immortal sea, forever. And they introduce you to a truly universal language.

INTERNATIONAL CODE OF SIGNALS

This is my all time favorite book on the stuff that the sea itself is all about. Everything can be said better with the aid of these signals. All you need to hold a long and involved and technical conversation between two ships or between ship and shore are a few flags or a flashlight. The nice thing is that you need not memorize anything. Get to know the system by which you look things up (ten minutes at most) and you can talk to admirals in their own language. The method that is outlined to deal with emergencies of every conceivable kind is worth its weight in gold.

RADIO NAVIGATIONAL AIDS

Radio-direction finding techniques, RDF stations, radio beacons, time signals, navigational warnings, distress signals, medical advice, long-range navigational aids, and radio regulations for marine stations. Volume A deals with the Atlantic and the Mediterranean. Volume B deals with the Pacific. Get familiar with the material, especially with the locations of aids to navigation and the Morse codes of the radio beacons. No need to memorize anything. You must only understand the systems and then you can, as I do, look things up as needed.

LIGHT LISTS

These are a sailor's bible. When you identify that Navlight for which you have been searching you know where you are. Learn all about lights. All about them, including all of the descriptive material accompanying each entry in this crucial volume. Know what is meant by range and period and pattern.

NAVIGATION RULES

You cannot just learn *about* this book. You cannot use this as a reference or as a guide. You must memorize this material. Plain old-fashioned rote memorization is what is needed so that, when you are at the helm and another boat bears upon you, you will know automatically how the skipper on the other boat will react to what you do and what actions will be expected of you.

WORLDWIDE MARINE WEATHER BROADCASTS

This is the communication side of weather forecasting and a description of the vast network by which weather statistics are gathered. The services described here will help you to avoid the typhoon that there is no need for you ever to be caught in.

That's it. That is your complete chart room. The irreducible minimum that you need to get your landlubberly head into a sealubberly mode. These selected charts and graphs and manuals will make a sailor out of you long before you step from the disarray of land to the contained orderliness of your little ship. But when you do, you will find that you will take your chart room, *in toto*, along with you. Once you have created your chart room you will never quit this magic place whose four close walls contain the oceans of the world. Your chart room is your first concrete step toward your own ocean passages. Build it. Stock it. Crawl into it and spend a year or so.

As a young man in Atlantic City, I was befriended by a most attractive young man. He was an artist, a painter, who had taken off for Europe after the war and having studied painting there, came home "to get ready to make my mark."

He moved into the basement of his folks' home and commenced preparing the space as a studio. Much wall painting and building was taking place as I left for school in New York. I returned some months later and found that my friend the artist had moved. I tracked him down to his new and larger quarters. He told me that working so close to his parents was stifling. He was busy rebuilding and decorating his new space to be ready to make his mark.

After some months I came to his studio once again and found that it was perfectly constructed as an artist's studio. My friend was busy preparing large canvases.

A year passed and when I returned to seek out my friend he was gone. Some investigation found him in the Village in New York. He was, when I visited him, building and decorating still another studio. "I left because, although it was almost ready, I felt disconnected from the art world. New York," he assured me, "is where it is at."

It took my friend another year to get his new studio in shape and as I was able to visit him now and then I found him again busily preparing canvases of which he now had scores stored in various stages. Five years passed and when I last looked in on my friend, he was still "getting ready."

The moral is clear. Get ready for the sea . . . but not over ready lest you, like my artist friend, never get to your dream out of fear that you are not ready enough.

THE TEN CLASSIC ERRORS

"What," a beginning sailor once asked me, "are the classic errors *everyone* makes?" The more I thought about that innocent question the more I realized that the same errors have been repeated by all of us *ad infinitum* and *ad nauseam* . . . Perhaps it is necessary to commit mistakes in order to learn to sail. Or perhaps, as Oscar Wilde stated, "Experience is the name everyone gives to their mistakes." Whether or not errors and mistakes are unavoidable, I prefer to think that some of you, more thoughtful than the herd, will heed my list of ten classic errors and save trouble, money, aggravation, and terror.

Not Knowing Your Boat

Sailors often take small sailing vessels on long passages without first acquiring that intimate knowledge of their boat which appears, reflexively and without thought, in emergencies. During emergencies there is no time to think, only time to react. An uninformed reaction can sink you, an informed one may save your life.

The best way to know your boat is to build her with your own hands. Then, whatever comes up, you have all the needed images ingrained into your head and the very feel of solutions in your fingers. Since few of us are either so lucky or so talented to be able to build, the next best thing, the closest approximation, is to commission her yourself. Then, upon taking delivery of your boat, tear her apart and, piece by carefully remembered piece, put her back together again. She is no Humpty Dumpty. She will survive the operation.

To know your boat, you must first know her bilge as well as you know the curve of your mate's behind. The bilge is the part of your boat that is most vulnerable and the least accessible. It is the place where accidents wait for inconvenient moments to happen. Move in for a week. Start from the bilge and work up.

Come to understand why the mast stays up. Become intimate with the tubes and valves that carry fluids throughout your boat. You must have a moving picture of your steering system in your head so that when something goes wrong (as it always does) at the wrong time (as it always does) you can view the solution in your head before you ever take wrench in hand. You must know the limits and strengths of your engine and the problems of fuel and of filtering and of water, bottom paint, electrolysis, and more. You must know your boat, her systems, capabilities and weaknesses, if you are to consider yourself a serious and responsible skipper.

Unscrew everything that will unscrew, search behind all paneling and headliners, disconnect and study your marine head until you can reassemble it in the dark, remove all deck fittings and add the proper backup plates your builder has overlooked. Reseal them with a good, expensive sealant which your stingy commissioner would not. You will be the one dribbled upon in a cold and wet bunk.

Know the exact locations of all the stores, spares, and emergency equipment you carry. You may have to get to the stuff quickly when the boat is half under water and halfway to her beam ends. There is no more satisfying act than to come to know the little vessel to which you are committing your life and safety and the lives of those whom you love.

Failure to Drill

Knowing precisely what to do when trouble arises is your first line of defense against disaster. The "what to do" about emergencies is contained in drills, of which there are only three: fire, man overboard, and abandon ship.

The drills are simple and direct but they must be practiced so that when an emergency arises, everyone aboard has enough information to avoid panic. Emergencies happen fast. They will overwhelm you unless you are drilled for knee-jerk responses.

FIRE DRILL

Fires happen and can kill with terrifying speed. A fire can sink your boat in five minutes. A five-minute fire drill can save both your boat and your life. All you really have to know is where the extinguishers are located and exactly how to send out a Mayday. Why gamble against odds like that?

ABANDON SHIP DRILL

Boats are not abandoned on warm, quiet, sunny days. If the time comes when you must consider an abandon ship order, you will be exhausted, cold, wet, and terrified. You may have been fighting wind and seas for hours, perhaps days, and be at the end of your emotional and physical tether. That is not the moment to learn how to unlash your liferaft or to wonder where the emergency rations are kept. It is vital to think clearly, in that moment of pure, anesthetizing panic, of the equipment and procedures you will need to survive.

MAN OVERBOARD DRILL

Do you know the sailorly techniques needed to return to an overboard crewmember from a reach or a beat or a run? Are you aware how quickly you lose sight of a person in even a moderate sea? And when you get back to your tired, scared, soggy, and perhaps unconscious crew, do you know how to retrieve him without further injury? If you can instantaneously answer all these questions (and a thousand more) then you are ready to go to sea. If not, you are at risk and the sea will find you out.

Failure to Reef

Sailors, seeking speed that cannot be attained by a displacement hull, put a damaging strain on their boats by carrying too much sail in too much wind. When you are overpowered everything is tossed about, everybody is wet and exhausted, and the boat ends up going measurably slower than it would were the rails high and dry out of the water. If anything is going to snap it will do so when the boat is overpowered and is already dealing with more wind than is comfortable. Not exactly the right moment to induce disaster.

Sea sense says that when you begin to think about reefing it is already too late. Shorten sail long before you approach the limits of control. There is a marvelous moment when, after being abused by too much wind and sea, you shorten sail and feel your boat settle down with a sigh of relief and a whispered "thank you."

Failure to Inspect

Nylon, Dacron, stainless steel, and fiberglass require scarcely any maintenance. But even these magic materials are subject to some physical deterioration. Lines chafe, sails break down from too much ultra-violet light, and stainless, when formed into useful shapes, can fatigue and develop mysterious cracks. Fiberglass, because of the fallible hands that lay it up, can work itself to death. Engines need oil, winches need grease, and those damned cotter pins keep falling out.

There is a three-word antidote to disaster about to happen: "Inspect-Inspect-Inspect." A famous solo sailor tells us of his morning constitutional. Before breakfast and before dealing with tasks clamoring for his attention, he walks his deck. Each morning he "circumnavigates" his craft, inspecting every cotter pin, every swage, the life lines, the lashings of deck carried stores and so on, port and starboard, bow to stern. After breakfast he repeats the same exercise below. He was impressed with how many small problems, predictive to major disasters, he was able to intercept. Failure to inspect is an invitation to exigency. Use all your senses. Feel, look at, and listen to everything on your boat. Try sniffing, too.

Relying on High-Tech Gear

High-tech is a fool's paradise. The first time I used a satellite navigation instrument, I put my feet up, closed my sight reduction tables, sealed up my sextant, and watched the little green stars march across the screen. What a relief from the gut-wrenching struggle to get a star sight from a lurching, bucking deck.

Then my SatNav conked out. Since that time I do not let a day go by at sea without, in addition to my GPS (which replaced my SatNav), a noon sight and a most carefully kept dead-reckoning log. Having two GPS's is one answer to the gremlins of technology. The ultimate answer is to know how to do without.

Reliance on high-tech equipment diminishes some of the very reasons we go to sea. The committed sailor finds a special joy in self-reliance, in taking neither aid nor assistance from anyone but himself. The sea is the last place on earth where we can still experience the thrill of accepting total responsibility for our lives. High-tech, like some soulless robot, wants to take that away from us.

I have no objection to a knotmeter so long as I know how to use a chip log, to a depthmeter so long as I can cast a lead, and I certainly have no objection to GPS so long as I can shoot a reasonably good noon sight (dead easy) with a sextant. I do object, however, to those fools who attempt to sail big oceans in little boats, relying on unrepairable equipment, and knowing little of the old fashioned, and simple techniques the high-tech stuff is designed to replace. When something goes wrong, and it always does, they find themselves in jeopardy and scream for expensive assistance.

Poor Anchoring Habits

Every sailor can tell you about the time the boat dragged the anchor down onto a sleeping neighbor or a lee shore. Without exception, we all, at one time or another, have felt our security evaporate as our anchor bounced like a balloon along the ocean floor. If every one's ground tackle has failed at some time, then it is clear that we are paying too little heed to getting our anchors down properly. It is not that sailors carry ground tackle that is too light for their craft. Usually the opposite is true. We simply fail to fully consider such boring matters as currents, tidal heights, and directions, and probable shifts in wind direction—all of which can seriously affect a boat bobbing at the end of half-a-hundred-weight of iron and half-an-inch of frangible nylon.

Worry about your anchor. Spend an extra half hour pulling and testing. Nag the hell out of it. Use your motor and your sails to try to pull it out of the ground from different directions, as surely the sea will try. Then, when you are satisfied, put on a snorkel and go down and look at it. Is it well hooked? Will the rode chafe? Will you be able to weigh it in the morning?

Practice anchoring. Practice dragging. Learn the pluses and the minuses of anchor types. Learn about holding ground and which kind each anchor prefers. Very small anchors have been known to hold very big boats in terrifying conditions. But the opposite is also true . . . so beware.

There cannot be any excuse for improper anchoring, it is simply bad seamanship. And never, never, never, cheat on scope!

Ignoring Weather Signs

Most events that can endanger your vessel are unlikely, rare, and improbable and require some conscious stupidity on your part. Weather, however, is neither rare nor unlikely and does not look to you for any assistance. All of the bad moments you will ever have on offshore passages will most probably be related to weather.

You cannot do anything about the weather, but if you are able to glean the slightest hint of what the weather is likely to be, you are in a position to measurably improve the safety of your vessel.

The sky screams its warnings and all you need do is stop, look, and listen. The dawning sky casts a shadow of the shape of the day's weather, and at dusk, the last glimpses of fading light hint at the nighttime changes the departing sun has prepared. At these moments all of your senses must be fully extended. Sight, smell, hearing, and touch all have their tales to tell. All is portent of what will happen.

Compare your own observations with the pilot charts, those impressive historical compendia of meteorological means and averages that define the horizons of your weatherly expectations. Pay close attention to your barometer which, since it delivers intelligence in relative rather than absolute terms, functions adequately even when slightly out of whack.

In addition to the sky, which does not get out of whack, there are sophisticated gadgets that do. The best of these is a good radio receiver (or two) that will plug you into weather frequencies around the globe.

Gadgetry aside, opt always for what the senses report and what the mind reflects. Pursue whatever advantage you can gain over Aeolus. He will kill you if you give him half a chance.

Lackadaisical Chartwork

The coastal and ocean charts we use today were laboriously laid down by brave men taking soundings from open boats in strange and foreign waters. The information remains remarkably accurate even after, in some cases, centuries. The sea is a paradox of ever-changing, never-changing movement, so that observations made long ago have an eerie, neoteric quality. Pay attention.

Marine charts, products of intensive and informed human labor applied over very long periods of time, are full of information. Winds, tides, currents, depths, bottom conditions, obstacles, dangers, lights, radio beacons, weather, and a thousand other pertinent facts are laid out on these powerful sheets. Yet sailors consistently fail to adequately chart courses, ignoring the wealth of information so readily available.

At moments when you have been too long abused by seas and winds and when the reality of your senses becomes distorted, your charts are the only reality left. Having marine charts and knowing how to use them is like inviting a host of old sailors to sail with you, share their experience with you. They recount their own passages in these very seas. They whisper in your ear, "Do this, do not do that, look out, look out," and always, "Be aware, be aware." Slocum heard their voices . . . you will, too, if you will only listen to your charts. You are in very good company.

The Captain Bligh Syndrome

A tired and hungry crew is an invitation to disaster. A crew that has not had its physical and emotional pelts stroked is a crew that can quickly get out of control. A sailor, who has spent precious off watch hours trying to sleep on a wet pillow because a leak was not attended to, will be cranky, angry, and inept. When you are tired, cold, and unloved, the most simple of tasks is like walking under water.

As a responsible skipper, you know that the safety of your boat depends upon the freely given cooperation of the crew. This cannot be demanded, it can only be politely requested.

So gently, skipper, gently, trod gently. For better or for worse your crew is all you have. Treat them with love, appreciation, understanding, and a good hot meal. They will return it all, and more, in kind.

The Worst Error

The worst error is to ignore these errors committed over and over by almost everyone. Training yourself to avoid these errors will not guarantee you safe passages, but careful attention to them is likely to short-circuit most catastrophe. Remember that ill luck is a commodity often manufactured by those upon whom it falls.

As for obstacles that you cannot foresee, you must trust in Providence for surely He must love sailors since He made us all so beautiful.

OFFSHORE WORTHINESS CHECKLIST

Before you can get into serious preparations for offshore passage making, it is prudent to take stock of the present condition of your boat and equipment and how much you actually know about both.

This checklist is designed to seek out the inadequacies of your boat and to define the dimensions of the task ahead of you. By completing it, you will become familiar with the basic physical requirements for an offshore passage. This list is an outline only. Much of this material will be dealt with later, some by reference to more knowledgeable sources. The checklist is merely a starting point, a test before the course. It is meant to plumb the lack, not the presence, of knowledge.

Do not depend upon good luck or a forgiving boat. Depend on your own close familiarity with your boat. Close familiarity is a precondition of offshore sailing. The longshore sailor can dump his problems in a marina. You cannot.

In order to help you through the list, hints and notations are included. These do not detail your needs nor do they suggest solutions. The hints are designed to indicate what you must look for and what you have yet to learn about.

Below Waterline Exterior

Osmosis. This is becoming pandemic among fiberglass boats. Pry with a screwdriver. Look for bubbles and soft spots.

Antifouling. Repaint your bottom just before departure. Match your antifouling paint to the waters in which you will be sailing. Any large paint manufacturer will be able to make the proper recommendation. Check on the latest information concerning tetracycline additives. Might save you a bundle.

Through-hull openings. Are they clear or blocked by marine growth? Is there any evidence of electrolysis? Where are they? Can you find them in the dark and under water?

Rudder. The rudder is the most probable underwater area to display osmosis—an early indication of trouble in your hull. Look for small openings into which water may have seeped along the trailing edge. Check the mounts for wear or cracks. Carefully inspect the rudder post through-hull bearing for looseness or leaking.

Instrument sensors. Log paddles should be free of growth and aligned fore and aft. The fathometer transponder should be deep and near the centerline. Is there any evidence of mechanical damage?

Electrolysis. Check your zincs. Are they eroded? Do you need more than one? Different boats have different areas where electrolysis shows up. Overzinc your boat just as you should oversize your rigging and overfilter your fuel.

Propeller. A nicked or damaged or bent prop can cost loss of speed and be the source of damaging vibration. This is usually obvious from visual inspection but very subtle and hard-to-observe alteration of shape may have occurred. Remove and have it checked by a prop shop when you do your antifouling.

Prop shaft. The portion of the shaft that is exposed outside the hull is subject to physical damage. Serious vibration can often be due to an out-of-line shaft. Any machining done on the shaft should be checked for *radius.* Ask your machinist what that means.

Below Waterline Interior

Through-hull valves. After a while they are a drag to open and close. Do you know how? In the dark, in a bad sea, up to your kazoo in freezing water is not the time to look for them. Locate each lever and diagram the location for the rest of the crew. Determine if they are all the same type and if they function similarly. If you have many differing types it might be best to standardize them. When through-hulls have to be closed at sea it must be done *now*.

Leaks. Even the smallest hint of unidentified incoming water below the waterline is an excellent reason for not setting out on an offshore passage. There will always be some salt water accumulation in the bilge. While at a dock close off all sweet water sources and time the rise of salt water intake. That will be your standard. Remember that underway you will be taking additional salt water from above and that seepage from below will increase due to warpage and stress. As long as intake is at the steady rate of flow that approximates your previously determined normal while the boat was at rest there is little threat. If the build up is variable or intermittent and if the source is not obvious, find and fix.

Mast base. Is it well seated and wedged? Is it evenly seated? Is it reasonably watertight at its entrance through the deck?

Chain plates. You might have to tear out some furniture to inspect these. Do it. Look for loosening or any evidence of movement. Also look for rust streaks that may indicate improper or inadequate bedding.

Engine mounts. Are they well fastened? Is there any evidence of shifting? Prod the rubber for freshness.

Stuffing box. Do you know how much water your stuffing box is *supposed* to leak? Monitor it for a couple of hours both at dock and under power. This will give you a reference.

Propeller shaft. Same inside as outside. Check lathe turning radii as the diameter of the shaft may have been turned down to fit the coupling to the engine. The cuts should be radiused, not sharp, right angles.

Above Waterline Interior

Deck leaks. Do what you can. You will not stop them all. At least be aware of the leaks you started out with so you will know when new ones appear. Moisture rarely appears below the area where the leak occurs. Water can seep a long way between decks before it falls in your ear.

Port light leaks. Check for warpage and gasket condition. Direct a strong stream of water externally.

Hatch leaks. Leaking hatches are unnecessary and correctable. Look first to the gaskets and then to the "dogs." Badly designed hatches are well worth replacing. If you cannot afford replacement, and they leak badly underway, seal them with a white silicone sealant while at sea and open them in port.

Dorade leaks. Dorades bring below only a smidgen of air and many seem perversely designed to more efficiently ship water than air. Check dorade design and function carefully at all angles of heel and then do what I did. Seal 'em up for the crossing.

Drawers and lockers. You want them to open and close when dry *and* when damp. I don't think anything is more aggravating than a jammed drawer. Are all lockers ventilated?

Floorboards. They must be free and easy to raise when dry *and* also when wet. Should you have to get to the bilge in a hurry, a floorboard swollen in place can be a big problem. Make sure that the floorboard lifting rings are through-bolted. I guarantee that yours are not.

Hull to deck and bulkhead joins. Tear out some furniture and inspect. You can learn more about the integrity of the boat here than anywhere. Athwartship bulkheads in fiberglass boats supply much needed stiffening. If they are not glassed to the hull, deck, and keel they can move and encourage structural failures throughout the boat.

Furniture. What is good enough longshore is simply not good enough offshore. Check for any sign of movement or loosened joints.

Standing Rigging

Swages. Use a magnifying glass and check for hairline cracks in the metal that is squeezed around the wire. Change to Norseman if you can afford it; repairs at sea will be easier. Stainless steel older than seven years is suspect.

Stays and shrouds. Use cotton gloves and wipe the whole length of each wire. You will discover if they need replacing as the glove catches on little slivers of steel. Replace any kinked wire. Kinks are unremovable. All wire rigging *must* be toggled wherever attached. When in doubt, a double toggle will not hurt. You can't be too thin, too rich, or toggle too much.

Turnbuckles. Check for damaged threads or *any* sign of physical damage such as bends in the sides or bends in the threaded rod. Make sure that the locking mechanism is positive, i.e. cotter pins rather than locking nuts.

Shackles. All shackles should be safety wired, preferably with Monel wire. Open and refasten all shackles before departure. You may have to get one off in a hurry, so make sure that none are seized or jammed. Replace all snap shackles with regular shackles or bowlines. Snap shackles are deceitful.

Masthead. Sheaves must run free with no sign of twist or strain. Pull out the sheaves and check the bearings for any sign of wear. Make sure that halyards run fair. Use plenty of toggles at the tangs. Unscrew VHF coaxial antenna lead, clean with sandpaper, and reconnect using plenty of sealant. Do the same for all electrical masthead connections. Replace all bulbs on masthead lights. Mid-ocean is no place to have your navlights bulbs blow.

Deck fittings. Must be through-bolted and adequately backed with stainless plates. They will be a source of leaks if badly bedded.

Running Rigging

Line. Get new line. Do not be chintzy. Limit variety of sizes and material. Use all Dacron, avoid nylon. Whip, do not burn ends. Burned ends increase the diameter at the end of the line and can lead to threading difficulties at awkward moments.

Shackles. Safety wire all shackles with Monel wire.

Fairleads. Fairlead blocks are subject to warping and damage. Are they adequate and the right size for your sheets? Deck-mounted, moveable fairlead blocks will beat themselves to death against the deck unless prevented.

Blocks. They need not be the expensive ball-bearing type. Old-fashioned solid bearings will do in most cases. Check all bearings for signs of wear.

Turning blocks. Subject to tremendous forces. Make sure they are adequate in size, fit your sheets perfectly, are most carefully fairleaded, and securely mounted with stainless steel backup plates.

Winches. Disassemble completely. Look for any sign of stress or internal wear or damage. Have plenty of spare pawls and springs. Lubricate, lubricate, lubricate. Only under the most extreme need should winches be disassembled at sea and then only if you are expert in keeping the little springs aboard.

Snap shackles. Sell them to a longshore sailor.

Sails

Fabric. Is the condition of the fabric and stitching adequate for offshore? Ask your sailmaker. Check for any signs of chafe. Attach sheets with bowlines in place of the snap shackles you took off. Keep all old sails as spares. Even new sails blow out.

Reef system. Before you leave, reef in the dark. Reef blindfolded. Reef with one hand tied behind your back. Reef when seasick, feverish, sleepy, or in love. If you do not have jiffy reefing, get it. Use three sets of reef points on your main and two on your staysail.

Safety Devices

Jackline (lifeline). Installed uninterrupted from bow to stern. Make it secure, easy to use and capable of attachment from the cockpit. Flexible wire is best.

Mast Rails. Should be installed high and secure with lots of places to tie things to, including yourself.

Safety harnesses. Different strokes for different folks so get lots of different styles. *They must be comfortable or they will not be worn.* Let the crew make their personal selection and identify with colored cord everyone's own harness.

Lifesling. The lifesling is a horseshoe-shaped flotation device attached with large D-rings to a floating line, 150 feet in length. Hang it on the stern pulpit.

Lifelines. Lifelines are dangerous to depend upon. Drill your crew to avoid their use for support especially in bad seas. Never attach safety harness to lifelines. Lifelines should be easily released to reduce freeboard in the event of a man overboard.

Spreader lights. They must be in working order, waterproofed as much as possible, and make sure you have spare bulbs. Do not use too bright ones. At sea at night a dim light will do as well as a bright one and will not blind the helmsman.

Liferaft, flares, and equipment. Flares must be updated regularly. Carry plenty of them since they are as often missed as seen. Equipment should include a short handled net and gaff as fish will not rise to hook and line but are easily gaffed as they gather under the raft for shade from the sun. Everything must be stainless.

Cooking Stove

Cooking gas bottles. Should be stowed outside so that potential leaks are fail-safe.

Propane fuel lines. Must be copper and soldered. Rubber tubing at the cooking stove, while necessary to allow movement of the stove, is a source of wear and trouble. The rubber hose should be clamped to the brass and fittings. This eliminates the hard spot, making the hose flex along its length. Automatic shut-off valves should be installed, along with a manual valve that should be shut down after each use.

Stove gimballing. Must be free and easy. Test for proper weighting and damping in deep heels. Gimballed stoves can jam at extreme angles. Test and check carefully: A stove jammed at an extreme angle can become dangerous as the boat turns to the other tack and the stove does not. At heel, with oven door open, check to see if stove remains level. If not, your dinner can land on your feet.

Stove rails. A must around burners. Are they high enough? Do they interfere with gimballing? You cannot have too many stove rails.

"Cook saver." This adjustable rig is designed to keep the cook close to but away from a hot stove. Allows hands-free cooking in an exuberant sea.

Bunks

Size. Make them long and narrow.

Bunkboards. Wood preferred, or canvas if you must. Make them high, adequate, negotiable, and comfortable.

Bunk location. High, warm, dry, and as much as possible out of traffic. The forepeak is no place for bunks for a sea-going vessel. During really bad times the cabin sole is the very best bunk.

Bunk leaks. The only place on a boat where leaks are *absolutely* and *totally* unacceptable is over bunks. Leaks are sleepkillers. They appear mostly under rough sea conditions. It is worth the effort to take your boat out in nasty weather and search out leaks beforehand.

Linen. Linen, like a safety harness, must be comfortable or it will do more harm than good. In chilly climes try flannel sheets; always use fitted sheets. Dryness comes before cleanliness.

Steering

Sheaves and cables. Check for distortion, for fairlead, and for the integrity of the attachment of sheaves to hull.

Rudder head. The point of attachment of tiller to rudder post is subject to great strain. If that goes, your steering goes. Inspect for wear.

Rudder post. Are there bearings installed at the through-hull and at the top of the post? Check bushings.

Rudder quadrant. Make sure that the steering cables lead fair to the quadrant and that it has not developed any twist. Carefully check the fastening to the rudder post.

Rudder bail. Do you have a stainless bail or a hole drilled through the trailing edge of the rudder? The best and cheapest emergency steering device ever invented.

Wheel gearing and wheel brake. Dismantle, inspect, and learn to reinstall. Remove the wheel brake altogether. It is not very useful on an offshore passage and is an unnecessary possible source of steering difficulties.

Emergency tiller. Find where your builder hid it and make it more available. Fit it to the rudder post and see if it is possible to use in heavy weather—or in any weather.

Autopilot. Takes tremendous stress offshore. Check the mount. Then remount the powering unit on the thickest steel armorplate you can find. You want no movement; it must be absolutely rigidly mounted.

Wind vane steering. A tradewind delight. It takes the strain off batteries, autopilot, and crew. It is useless longshore. The best are mechanical servo devices operating directly on your steering system. However, as with all else, anything will work, even rubber tubing and lines between the jib and the wheel.

Anchor Systems

Bow anchors. Are they adequate weight for the boat? Get at least one that is heavier than you will ever think you will need. You will need it. Use CQRs and Danforths only. *Original* CQRs and *original* Danforths. No copies allowed. The copies may be almost as good, but in anchoring there is no "almost." Many experts now recommend Bruce. I avoid new and experimental anchors. Let others do R&D. Eschew the beautiful stainless anchors. They twist up like pretzels.

Stern anchor. Every boat should have one *and* a stern rode locker.

Chain. For a 40-foot boat, the chain should be 10mm (3/8") proof coil, and carefully matched to your windlass gypsy. Get 300 feet. You'll need it.

Rode. Use fat nylon. Is it stored separately from the chain? Do you have more than you will ever need? You'll need it.

Rode lockers. Rode and chain must fairlead and stack in lockers without tangle. Are the lockers low enough? Are they as far aft as you can reasonably locate them? Consider a little re-designing to get the weight of chain as low and as far aft as possible.

Windlass and gypsy. Proof coil chain will properly fit the correct gypsy. Unproofed chain won't, and it will break your fingers when anchoring. Check electrical power cable to the windlass.

Bow rollers. An endless source of trouble in uncomfortable anchorages, of which you will have many in a worthwhile offshore passage. Test in all kinds of weather and seas. Most of the problems can be obviated by the use of a turtle, sometimes called a false rode.

Instrumentation

Wind instruments. Nice to have. Nice if they work. But you can live without them when they go belly-up. Davis makes a cheap backup.

Water speed. Are you backed up with a Walker (taffrail) log? Port and starboard mounts should be installed. A Walker is cheap and always works (when a shark doesn't take the spinner) and is remarkably accurate. Lots around secondhand. You will eventually be able to guess your water speed to half a knot.

Navigation

Celestial. Easiest to learn and most reliable. It still is—and always will be—a fundamental requirement for the offshore sailor.

Electronic. GPS, the nicest thing since sex and less trouble. The newer models seem much more reliable and the handheld models are too good to be true.

Compasses. Are they corrected? Do they agree? Do you have several? Is the area around the compass ferrous free and free of radios, etc.?

Electrical Systems

Alternators. Two belted to the engine would be best. Is there room to belt an alternator to your prop shaft? Can you replace a belt in the dark? Underwater, etc.?

Generators. You need a pretty big boat to require a diesel generator. Under 40 feet heave it overboard. Over 40 feet the only way to go is with a small diesel driven 12-volt model built by Balmar. If you need 110 or 220, get an inverter.

Alternative electrical supply. Sun, wind, water, gasoline, or diesel. You should have some alternative source offshore.

Batteries. Can be too big as easily as too small. Too big and you will never keep them filled. Too small and they may not start your engine. Match your alternator output to your battery capacity. Mounting must be secure. I have seen lightly secured batteries leap up, up, and away in a bad sea. Know the location; it must be available for checking. The weight distribution must be low but out of bilge water.

Wiring. The diameter of the wire installed on your boat is too small. It is always too small. The only thing small wire does efficiently is change electricity into useless heat that sometimes can burn up your boat. Starter motors and windlasses need the heaviest cable. Crimped joins can be as good as soldered, but crimped and silver soldered is the best answer to stopping corrosion. Your grounding connections are as important, or maybe even more important, than your positive leads.

Communication Systems

Very high frequency. Nice to talk to passing ships. Check quality of coaxial cable. Copper sheathing must be generous. VHF is generally useless offshore but becomes important as harbors are reached.

High frequency SSB. Amateur or Marine SSB. Amateur is better and cheaper but you have to know a bit about radio.

Cellular and satellite. The newest wrinkles. Cellular is nifty along shore. The usefulness of satellite in emergencies is limited.

Alphabet flags. My favorite form of marine communication. Throw away the little ones. Get big ones.

Exotica. Noise, light, smoke, Morse, fireworks, guns, and yelling into a loud hailer.

Water Systems

Water pipes and valves. Get to know them. Replace hose clamps whether they need it or not. Double clamp them. Nylon valves are nifty.

Filtration. As with fuel, the more water filtration the better. Double filter on every line.

Water tankage. Multiple small tanks prevent loss or fouling of all your water supply.

Emergency water. Discrete, emergency tankage. Hand-operated, reverse osmosis device. Floating rubber balloon stills. Squeeze a fish.

Fuel Systems

Fuel lines and valves. Trace, replace, maintain, and monitor. Do it in the dark. Do it.

Fuel filtration. The more the better. Get the best and get plenty. Double filter. Triple filter.

Fuel tankage. Again, multiple small tanks prevent loss or fouling of your fuel supply.

Fire Prevention

Portable extinguishers. Spend the money and get plenty. Make sure that extinguishers are located so that you will not be cut off from them by any possible fire.

Automatic installations. Mount a large automatic fire extinguisher unit over your engine and batteries. Every offshore boat should have at least one large automatic extinguisher in the engine room.

There you have it. These are the basics. Learning is a growth process. You have already learned a little from merely scanning this list even if you are now confused and a little discouraged by the mass of stuff that you should get through if you want to get out there. Slow accretion of knowledge happens until, suddenly, without conscious effort, you find yourself on a new plateau with new vistas and perspectives. That is what "Gestalt" means. It is the closing of the circle of understanding so that you are ready for the next, larger circle.

CHAPTER 3

Getting Crew

PLANNING FOR A GOOD CREW

While there are ancient and accurate charts of the sea that tell in exquisite detail what you may expect in all the great oceans, after a thousand generations of humanity, there still are no guidelines to determine whether the crew you are signing on be devils or angels.

The fact is that you do not want either devil or angel. Too good can be as exasperating as too bad. What is needed on a small boat over a long passage is someone whose faults are mildly attractive and whose good qualities do not cause your own to suffer by comparison.

Acceptable crew is a vital part of your offshore adventure. It is unlikely that the sea itself will kill you, but it is very likely that a sour, petulant, and lazy watchmate can make you wish you were dead. After elysian visions of passage, a belching, farting, snoring, lazy lout in the next bunk can turn dreams to dross. Trial passages tell you no more about what evil lurks in the heart of crew than does your first impression. The bad stuff and the good stuff in them appears, as if on schedule, five days out and five hundred miles downwind.

Every crewmember comes with a bundle of emotional problems, an aeolian box of miseries that you will get to open when it is too late to do anything. Since it has not been established that any one human being is really any better or any worse than any other, the only way to deal with crew is to admit that they are as bad as you are. Then you can accept their foibles with as much forgiveness as you grant your own. Since you have not been able to change yourself very much throughout your life, it is unlikely that you will be able to reform another person during the month or so that you will be together.

To Pay or Not to Pay

Before you get down to the business of acquiring crew you must be very clear about financial arrangements with them. There are three ways to go: paid crew, unpaid crew, and paying crew. All arrangements are full of problems, but the only alternative to these three is to sail alone. I have queried many solo sailors as to why they indulge in their lonely madness and the invariable answer is to avoid the bother of dealing with crew. In general, taking on crew carelessly is like marrying in haste. It can be followed by long periods of repentance.

PAID CREW

With real sailors, and paid crew usually fall into that category, the great and overriding drive is the desire to be passaging. If you go with paid crew you may expect more of them than of unpaid crew because they are committed to the sea, not because you are paying them. If both you and your paid crew are competent skippers, there may be a trial of wills that, if not set right, can unsettle the passage. There can only be one skipper and that must be you.

How much you must pay for crew is a balance of their experience, your negotiating skills, and how badly they want to go sailing. The going wage, including room and board and one round-trip home a year, is generally about half the average landbound income.

I only hired paid crew for my first ocean passage, the crossing of the Stream from Fort Lauderdale to the Bahamas. I was so new to sailing in my Westsail 32 that this handful of miles was fraught with all sorts of imagined dangers. It was the single most valuable experience in my sailorly life not only for what he taught me but because he helped me to realize that the skills I needed to sail oceans, mysterious as they seemed, were more easily achieved than I had ever imagined.

He was an airline pilot who loved to sail. He used his layover times to hire himself out, not so much for the money, as pilots are well paid, but for the pure love of sailing. My luck was that he was a good sailor and a great teacher; and he loved to do both equally. He recognized early how little I knew and instead of burdening me with a show of all that he knew, and thus perhaps dissuading me from the sailorly life, he chose only one aspect of navigation which so often is overlooked in this age of electronics and deprecatingly misunderstood by beginning sailors. He taught me dead reckoning. When the brilliance of that technique burst into my darkened mind, a sailor was born.

UNPAID CREW

The second possibility is crew who will sail with you for fun only. These folk tend to be your emotional colleagues. They are probably out there for the adventure, the same as you are. Unpaid crew can be drawn from a larger sample than any other thus making it a bit more likely to match your needs and prejudices. They are considerably less permanent, less reliable, and more likely to jump ship than paid crew.

Unpaid crew will cost you more than just for food since they will be your companions ashore as well as aboard, and it is proper for you to pay their way on excursions, and at restaurants and the like. They also will be entitled to an allowance for boat-related clothing items.

PAYING CREW

The least attractive arrangement is crew that will pay *you* for the privilege of sailing. I have never known a good outcome from taking paying crew aboard. I once witnessed the arrival of a boat in the harbor of Galle in Sri Lanka. The anchor was no sooner in the water than the crew, all paying their way, erupted from the boat in their haste to be away. The divergence of stories, from the skipper on one side and the crew on the other, would have been hilarious had the tellers not been in such emotional pain. Most of the complaints from the skipper were about a gluttonous, disobedient crew, and from the crew about a parsimonious and drunken skipper.

Aside from the legal problems of liability, paying crew feel that they have rights that non-paying crew and paid crew do not have. They come close to being passengers and we all know what kind of troubles that can lead to. However, if you need the money, it may be the only way to go.

Crew Travel Arrangements

Whatever your financial arrangements, you must be very clear on who pays for travel to and from the boat. Have crew sign an agreement and make sure that you cover unpleasant contingencies such as terminating crew in a foreign port. The best method for efficiently disposing of inadequate crew is to require that they possess a paid return ticket when they sign on, lest you have to pay their fare home as the local gendarmes required of the outraged skipper in Sri Lanka.

Length of Sign on for New Crew

Sign on all crew for short passages only. Never sign on crew without agreeing over the place or time of termination. Crew that must be terminated midway in your voyage are a source of continuing aggravation even after you have decided to be rid of them. After this first short leg, if the crew does not work out, you have lived up to your contract with them and they should have no beef. On the other hand, should your crew turn out to be swell, as all of mine were, you have the happy option of signing them on again.

GETTING CREW

The stages in the development of crew for a long passage are:

Recruiting

Interrogating

Choosing and *living with your choice*

These are gray divisions. Sometimes they all happen at once. Other times some are skipped. A good deal of the time you awake with crew who, as with a hangover, you have only the haziest recollection of how you came by them.

Recruiting

RECRUITING BY ACCIDENT

In the long run this is probably the best way to recruit. Cyndee did a bikini bounce down the dock in Panama and asked all in one deep breath if we were going to Tahiti and could she come along. All of our male chemicals agreed without investigation or reservation. She came on board *sans* experience, *sans* reference, *sans* anything save a bosun's knife, bubbly enthusiasm, and a bikini. She remained for five years, married my mate, and left with all passionately in love with her, not with her figure, but with the strength and the consistency of her spirit.

It was a high risk with a happy ending. I have tried listening to my chemistry on other occasions, not always with such marvelous luck. But accidental acquisition is not a bad way to go. Most folk are fundamentally the same, so what you stumble over the first time around is likely to be as good as what you might agonize over.

RECRUITING BY MEDIA

Try the conventional means of placing or answering ads in sailing magazines. Nothing much will come of it. But at least this experience will give you a wider understanding of what kind of ding-a-lings want to go sailing and will cause you to be less critical of the real sailors you might come across. Folk who advertise for berths usually have a fixed segment of time available. They want to depart and return on specific dates that might well not fit your needs. Few media ads are open-ended regarding times of passage and, for this reason alone, soliciting by media is problematical at best.

The best media ad is the bulletin board in the marina or harbor in which you happen to be. Most people who place or answer such ads at least know the pointy end from the other end and, by their mere presence near the sea, have already made a commitment of sorts.

RECRUITING FRIENDS

Very, very dangerous. The guy with whom you have pleasantly played poker for years may have an *idée fixe* concerning the nature of your relationship that simply will not work at sea. The nifty gal whom everybody likes may find that close confines and limited social contacts are different than being part of a larger crowd. It is better, far better, to develop a new relationship with crew at sea than to try to transfer to your boat relationships that have worked on land. And that goes for relatives, too.

Interrogating

During interrogation try to discover how folk will wear on you in close quarters over a long time. Watch what they do and how they act rather than what they say. Everyone is on best behavior in an interview and your impressions must account for their desire to please.

Let the interview continue over a meal and, if possible, over as many days as you or the interviewee have free. Be in no hurry, it takes time to winkle out personality quirks. It will be the very small things, the faults of personality, rather than the larger skills and experience that will make or break a passage. Should you find someone you really like but whose skills and experience are limited, take them on and teach them. You cannot change personality but you can share knowledge.

In the final analysis a calming, or disquieting, feeling in your belly is as good an indicator as anything.

UNACCEPTABLE CREW

There are some problems that you must not take on. There are some habits that are destructive, first to the user and then ultimately to others in the crew. Here are a few "bewares."

Smoking Crew. Make nonsmoking a prerequisite and you will automatically reduce problems with nonsmokers by half. If you are a smoker yourself, take anyone you like . . . but not me.

Addicted Crew. Beware of dopers. These folk are big trouble, not only because they snort or smoke, but because they likely will bring dope aboard. Should your boat be caught with even a token amount of drugs in some ports, you will find your butt in the pokey and your boat up for auction. To make matters worse, addicts have been known to support their habit by dealing and may well use your innocent sailboat for a spot of smuggling. If you have any suspicions after sign on, you have a perfect right to search their belongings. If you find *anything* at all, deep-six it immediately and offload the offender at the nearest port.

Alcoholic Crew. Beware of heavy drinkers. Everybody takes a drink. A bottle of rum, some good wine, and a case of beer are the natural stores of a convivial boat. But not too convivial. Heavy drinkers will rarely pull their own weight so carefully ration and control the flow of alcoholic beverages while aboard. Avoid signing on heavy drinkers in the first place, but should you discover after sign on that you have alcoholics among your crew, send them packing at the first opportunity.

References and Resumes. References can be both important and misleading. No one likes to speak ill of either the dead or the absent, especially in writing, so references are likely to gloss. *Be careful of resumes with large gaps of time.* Who knows what was going on during those blank periods that prospective crew are wary to reveal.

Choosing and Living with Your Choice

Having avoided smokers, dopers, and alcoholics, you now must live with the choices that you have made. Any attempt to seriously change how a person acts and reacts is feckless and unrewarding. Even you, perhaps, cannot stop smoking and I certainly keep letting out my waistline. Why should we expect that others, neither better nor worse than ourselves, could change their way of living for the sake of 30 days at sea? We all are made up of good and bad traits. Some more and some less acceptable to a skipper choosing a crew. There will be no perfect crew so there will be no perfect choice. At best your crew will be no more perfect than you.

Once the seeking and the questioning is behind you, make a choice and accept it fully. Those you choose deserve that you accept, without reservation, both them and the choice that you have made. If you have reservations about your choices the passage will be a disaster. Be determined that you will like and admire your crew and thus make it difficult and ungracious for your shipmates to disappoint your high hopes for them.

Complete approval of crew is the ultimate method of assuring good passages. Disapproval always returns disapproval. Approval is neutral, and besides it feels good.

HIRING THE HANDICAPPED

What handicaps people is our view of them. To me, a lad who cannot read is handicapped. To the lad, that I cannot shinny up a rope makes me a cripple.

The human animal is inheritor of ten thousand talents of which he may master no more than a few. Any absent talent makes you, like a one-armed sailor, handicapped. Our greatest geniuses, those who have writ and rewrit human history, were all lousy at something. Freud cannot be thought of as a stand-up comic, nor can Einstein be pictured shinnying up a rope. Whatever we are handicaps us for whatever we are not. The blind, the lame, the deaf, the dumb, the young, the old, the female, and the mentally ill are all "handicapped" when compared to the sighted, the limbed, the hearer, the talker, the old, the young, the male (in our skewed culture), and to whatever presently passes for the sane.

All of us are little more than an amalgam of handicaps. A one-legged man on Fifth Avenue at rush hour is at a disadvantage. Put him in his own home, a smaller world adjusted for his absent leg, and his disadvantage diminishes. Put him on his own small boat, where suddenly *he* is his own universe, and *you* become the handicapped.

The only difference between those with a handicap and those without is the dimension of time. Given time to explore the environment, the blind can see as well as sighted colleagues. Given time, a one-armed climber can, and has, scaled the Matterhorn, and given enough time, peg-leg Tristan Jones sailed twice around the world before you would have sailed twice around Long Island.

Sailors know that one of the unexpected gifts of sailing is endless time. Nothing has to be done in the imperious "now." On a forgiving boat—anything else is unconscionable abuse— you will rarely be required to do nothing more quickly than get to the head after a sip of the curious brew they call water in the Galápagos. You can take a week to wait out a fog, a couple of days to carefully reconnoiter a new harbor entrance, and you should long since have cleverly reefed in anticipation of the squall that will probably miss you anyway. An offshore sailboat is the very definition of lenity. Nothing is sudden, all is forgiven and, given time, what you do badly can be done all over again. Does that not sound like just the very place for all us handicapped folk? You bet it does.

The Handicap of Being Female

There are more women out there sailing their own boats these days. They are, on some kind of average, better sailors than men. The perceptual problems that exist concerning women on small vessels have nothing to do with those women who skipper their own vessels. They know their own minds. They are sailors and are sailing because they want to sail.

Skippers aside, there are two other kinds of female crew: women who would genuinely rather not be sailing but who sail only because their mate does, and women who have been culturally conditioned to believe that "sailing is not for ladies," but are doing it anyway. Both sail out of some sense of duty and this is a pity. Neither they nor the men with whom they sail can be comfortable with a crew who suffers as a duty what should be enjoyed as a delight.

Both the women who sail because their men want them to and those who claim they will not sail no matter what, have been subjected to the same male-dominant impositions that erroneously dictate that a lady cannot fix cars and toilets. Too many women live lives defined for them, not lives they might freely choose for themselves. Ultimately this is what keeps women from the sea.

If you are a man and want to sail with a woman, you must help her to confront, head on, this imposed sense of female inadequacy. She must know that there is nothing that a man can do aboard a sailing vessel that she cannot do as well and there are some things she can do a lot better. Most women sailors do not yet believe this and, in some cases, a male skipper finds that her fears about herself are a comfort to his manly self-image.

As skipper it is your primary obligation to disenchant any feeling of incompetence by forcing upon her all tasks that happen aboard. She must learn the sea and the vessel, as you did, by the doing. She must know that nothing is beyond her abilities and that your Olympian command of your boat and the sea rests on a mere few months more of hands-on experience than she has had.

When it comes to sailing a small boat on a long offshore passage, being female is a curable handicap. The medicine is simple, honest concern. The doctor is the skipper to whom she has mysteriously and lovingly bonded herself not only as crew but as lifemate.

Jenny came aboard for an Atlantic crossing as a somewhat bemused appendix to her week-old bridegroom. Brian had built himself a sailboat in which he tooled about on day sails off the southern coast of England. His dream was to do a circumnavigation with his new bride. When they joined us, he was gung-ho and she was not quite certain upon what she was embarking.

The gung lasted until the first dawning when Brian turned green. Stick-on patches, copper bracelets and pills did no good and poor Brian weakened steadily for the entire 28-day passage. Meanwhile Jenny grew stronger each day. In the rolly-polly of the passage she could read, sew and knit, loved to go below to do galley duty, and baked our bread for the passage. She handled sails, worked the foredeck and, as a blessed bonus rarely found in either male or female crew, chatted only when chatted at. She became that most precious of shipmates, an amiable, amenable, effective and silent sailor.

As Brian's dream of distant fabled seas evaporated in nausea, we could see a small cloud looming on the horizon of their marriage. She, not he, was the sailor. She, not he, had a circumnavigation in her future.

Marilyn, now my wife, who, when we married declared that this was her first marriage and my last, had never set foot on a sailboat when I phoned her from Senegal. I needed a companion to sail the Atlantic in my 32 footer. Knowing her to be accommodating and decorative, I invited her to come along. Accommodating, yes. Decorative, yes. But packed into that small and delicious frame was a will that kept this tyro of a skipper going through bad seas and ignorance.

We were three aboard. Marilyn often doubled at the wheel and always in the galley. As the seas piled up her eyes widened in disbelief but never a word of dismay or recrimination. I knew I had a winner when, on her first dark and windy night at sea, the moon surged out from clouds behind her with the intensity of a searchlight from hell. Although she was terrified to turn and see what the infernal brightness might be, she stood her paralyzed ground, never giving way to the terrors she must have felt.

And then the scenario screamed into the improbable as an invisible flying fish thrust by a rising wind from a white-capped sea whipped aboard and slapped her across the face. I would have fainted. She did not. She married me in spite of knowing that she would certainly be required to double not only at the wheel and in the galley, but in my life itself.

The Handicap of Being a Kid

Our world has been functionally atomized. We accept culturally assigned roles that deprive us of broader experiences. Old folk may not do this, and women may not do that, and kids, the most deprived of all, are presently assigned the role of doing practically nothing. Other than a loose and undisciplined obligation to school, kids have little defined relationship to the "real" world in which their parents live. They derive most of their life experience from peers who have as little experience as they do. They feed on the thin adolescent gruel of half-understood sensations of sex, drugs, and rock and roll, all of which may be O.K. in the larger perspective, but kids, banned from the real world, are without understanding of this larger perspective.

Kids survive this handicap, but at an emotional price that results in troubled adulthood. There are no free rides, and when a kid has not been taught to be responsible and involved, there is no reason to expect that responsibility to automatically appear in the child-become-adult.

The sea change, that mysterious process of growth and accommodation, has its greatest impact on children. Life aboard the tiny universe of a sailboat on a long passage converts a kid from a dysfunctional mote to a crucial and necessary part of the survival of the vessel. Kids remain kids only in size . . . in function they stand tall alongside their parents, where they have wanted to be all along.

What a marvelous gift, what a life's lesson, an offshore passage is for a child who has been deprived of hands-on reality. It is the ultimate that parents have to offer to a kid, a chance to share in the real world of work and survival. This sharing cannot happen in the crowded and shattered world of land and it cannot even happen on short and discontinuous passages longshore. It can only take place after you will have been weeks at sea together, weeks dependent for survival on your commitment to each other. Watch your kids grow as you delight (my grandfather of blessed memory would have said *qvell*) in their accomplishments.

The Real Handicaps

PHYSICAL HANDICAPS

It would be tiresome to list the sailors who have conquered the sea half-sighted, unhearing, *sans* arms or *sans* legs. It is only on solo passages, which should be abjured, that absent limbs become important. While a one-armed solo crew is diminished by half, the vessel with four crew aboard is diminished by only one-eighth, seven arms being only marginally less useful than eight. The central lesson that an offshore passage teaches is that it is the sum, not the exclusions, of abilities that lead to successful and joyful passages.

The crew of the aptly named *Outward Leg* had only three legs (subsequently reduced to two) out of the normal four, and the yacht *Trishna*, a lovely Swan 35 peopled by six Indian Army artillerymen, has an unlegged crewman. When we met Tristan on *Outward Leg* in Rhodes, he had just sailed and portaged across the spine of Europe. When we met *Trishna* in Port Sudan, with a crew that had never been offshore (Indians rarely sail), she was ebulliently embarked, *sans* experience and two legs, on the difficult passage from England to Bombay.

MEDICAL HANDICAPS

Chichester, on his last solo voyage, when he was dying of a painful cancer, had the last of his many laughs at the world when he achieved his long sought-after 200 miles noon-to-noon. He might have stayed home and died without it but, if he had, he would have come up one laugh short.

Going to sea with a serious medical handicap is a judgment call. A sailor with a history of heart attacks and the promise of more, may find the option of going toes-up at sea to be much more attractive than cold bedpans, lugubrious physicians, and weepy relatives. Having the option of how and where we die has to do with the quality not the quantity of life, and a sailor on borrowed time can accomplish more real living at sea in days than he can on land in months.

A medical handicap that winds itself slowly down to the patient's death, rather than into some institutional extension of minimally being alive, should not keep a committed sailor ashore.

The only thing that modern medicine has been able to do is to marginally improve the quality of life, not its length. Improving quality is no trick. Every sailor knows what improves the quality of life. We need no complicated econometric study to prove what our senses croon to us each moment at sea.

From the skipper's point of view, crew who could shuffle off this mortal coil might be a better risk than they appear at first glance. Chances are that death will not happen during the passage, if only because everybody is having so much fun. Chances are that the moribund one will do the deed in a hospital where the statistics have proven that it should be done. During the passage, the prospect of imminent demise may well make a better human being out of both the patient and the rest of the crew. The imminence of death has always been held to improve character.

EMOTIONAL HANDICAPS

From amongst the dizzying litany of mental illnesses, only a paranoid is impossible to sail with. We are all a little crazy anyway, so whatever crew is chosen will likely be no worse than the skipper. In the eyes of landlubbers, sailors are all out-to-lunch for even considering an offshore passage, and maybe they are right.

If you insist on totally normal folk, whatever that is, you will either never be satisfied with the selection available, or you will have a deadly dull crossing. On an offshore passage you will spend a long time unable to escape from the few people who should have been chosen for the likelihood that they might bring some fresh cheese to the table. Go with the Don Quixotes of the world, they may be a helluva lot of trouble, but they make dynamite copy.

THE HANDICAP OF AGE OR OLD SAILORS NEVER DIE

Ben Franklin, who himself lived to a great and verdant age, was once asked by a young man for advice on the choice of a mistress. Being a moralist, old Ben suggested that it would be better to wed but, being a realist, he advised the young man to take an old mistress rather than a young one.

Ben argued that an old mistress had: (1) wide knowledge of the world and could be helpful to a young man's career, that (2) age replaces mere vanity with the desire to improve character, that (3) she had acquired great experience and that (4) she was both more prudent and more protective of the reputation of her paramour, and that (5) anyway a young woman is as likely to be made miserable as an old woman is to be made happy and that (6) *"lastly,* [old mistresses] *are so grateful"* (*Reasons for Preferring an Elderly Mistress*, 1765).

Ben's advice is as compelling for signing on old sailors as it is for bedding older women. Old sailors have gained wide knowledge of the world, have little to be vain about, have great experience of the sea, are prudent and protective, can be easily made happy and, lastly, they are *so grateful.*

Should skippers be doubtful of the physical abilities of old sailors they need only to skim the literature of the great passages. Ancient mariners litter the seas of the world, pushing their boats, as slow and creaky as they themselves, across great oceans. Sailing is a game invented for dotage. Great muscle is infrequently required and speed never.

Grand climacteric sailors should be sought out and welcomed by young skippers for all the reasons given and for one more which old Ben had the delicacy to skip: professional technique. In both lovemaking and sailing, technique and touch and instinct, all honed by use, can best be acquired from the previous generation, be they lovely old ladies or salty old men.

THE SEAMAN'S BESTIARY

Of the entire zoological range available as crew, all are, in their own way, equally delightful to be with. By whatever standards, dogs as crew are better than people. And so are cats and birds and monkeys, and anything else that has the blessed inability to speak. Animals rarely have an opinion on sail trim that aggravatingly differs from the skipper's.

That does not mean that animals are not good listeners. They are superb listeners and will lie at your feet drinking it all in for as long as you wish to pontificate. Even after a month or so, when the more lingual crew has been known to throw themselves over the side rather than listen once more to tales of your love life, your dog will even continue to pant a little as you get to the juicier bits.

Cats seem not to be as good listeners since they have the talent to do other things while being regaled. A cat will either sleep or lick herself, both of which activities are likely to suggest that you are not getting her entire attention. However, a purr at the right moment is sometimes as good as a pant.

Some, like the pig, may be a bit too equal and some, like the horse, may not fit in the foc'sle. But from among all those creatures who do fit, there is certainly more than one silent, adoring, and non-demanding creature who will more perfectly key to your own profile of idiosyncrasies than will any human. Whichever the animal, it will demonstrate a loyalty that will make the grudging acquiescence of the rest of your crew seem, by comparison, mutinous.

For sailors with a practical turn of mind there are the birds. Hens are nice because they supply eggs and protein if you have the stomach. A brace of pigeons of the homing variety will bring help if you can stay afloat long enough for them to get home. A pelican, whose bill can hold more than his belly can, might be signed on for his skill as a fisherman. A ribbon tied loosely around the pelican's neck will prevent fish in his bill from becoming fish in his belly. A bit unfair, perhaps, but the pelican will love you none the less for it. Try that on a two-legged crew and see what happens.

Snakes immediately head for the bilge from which you can rarely entice them for a chat and holding a conversation with your bilge is liable to panic your crew. Turtles are dull and, while a pet rat is nice, you would probably have to choose between it and your wife.

From among this vasty bestiary, available to the mariner as taciturn crew, it all comes down to Man's Best Listener. True, dogs do have a few habits which cannot be trained out of them. Some tend to be a bit flatulent (but so are you), some drool too enthusiastically when showing affection (but so do you), some shed and some may be a bit too jealous but, all in all, dogs, as crew, are the best beasts.

In addition to scratching your lonely bone, dogs serve serious purposes aboard a small boat. They are the watch that never sleeps and will, in port, loudly announce the approach of friend or foe. Any dog bigger than a bread box is sufficient to dissuade strangers and alert the neighborhood; they will defend you to the death.

Disposal of doggy-do is no problem since dogs are easily trained to "do" in a delegated place at a delegated time. Even an old dog can be taught this new trick and a pup is a cinch. The only thing you cannot teach a dog to do is hang his rear-end over the rail and, in all fairness, I do not know many sailors who have mastered that technique. At any rate, do not allow the small problems of personal puppy hygiene deny you the pleasure of having a dog aboard, especially since he would rather be with you than anywhere else in creation. One *caveat* . . . If you are headed toward England, beware of their extreme animal quarantine laws. Best to check quarantine laws wherever you are headed.

I have not carried a beast aboard and I realize that I am missing much. The one time that I did rub up against an animal was memorable and, though bittersweet, delicious. We were enjoying the effusive Japanese hospitality of the Kansai Yacht Club near Kobe when a sorry, sick, and bedraggled kitten wandered aboard. Our human crew immediately turned into sentimental wrecks, and for three days we fed, ministered to, and monitored the poor tyke until she quietly gave up her tiny little ghost. We found a small rise at the sea's edge where we buried her. She had been with us only three days and, beast though she was, she gave us the most human of all of our moments of passage.

By all means take an animal as crew. They are, perhaps, God's apology for all the human assholes in the world.

CHAPTER 4

Life Aboard

The Sun will rise tomorrow without your assistance.

MAX PALLEY

The sea is the ultimate destroyer of slothful habits of land. On a small boat all comfort to which you have become accustomed is reft away. Support systems disappear and what you do not do for yourself does not get done.

The sea forces you to use your body. Your body is in endless motion every moment that you are at sea. Your muscles are at work merely to keep you quiet, and should you have to move, and move you must to eat and to live, the effort is nearly constant.

It is thus that the sea makes your body work.

The sea dishabituates you of boredom and depression. On a small vessel you are so busy being and doing that boredom becomes a condition only dimly remembered, perhaps even yearned for. When, with your own hands because there are no others, you splice a wire, grease a winch, sew a sail, or cook a meal, you retrieve a glorious sense of self-worth so easily blunted by the ductile delights of land.

There are a thousand ways that the sea unclenches the enthralling grip of land. In the planning, preparing for, and actually doing of a long offshore passage, society's fist of restraint opens until it becomes merely a palm in which you nestle to regain your life. It is in the simple things required of you aboard and denied you on land that the lessons of emancipation and self-respect first appear. How you victual your boat, the kinds of foods you take aboard, how you relate to their preparation, how you clean (or foul) your nest, and how you intervene to keep your little universe afloat, are all part of the grand process of recapturing your soul. These are the disciplines of self-respect that an ocean passage demands of us. These are the destroyers of bad habits. The sea change cannot happen on land. It will not fail to happen to you at sea.

VICTUALING: AN EXERCISE IN AESTHETICS

Victualing is the ancient term for provisioning a ship with food and drink. It is essentially an aesthetic matter, and those who have passaged on small boats for long periods understand that how you feel about food at sea is every bit as important, and perhaps more so, than its variety, its quality, and its ability to nourish you.

The use of low-energy foods on a long passage is to be desired for many reasons. High-energy foods such as meat and fish are unpleasing to the ambiance of a small boat. Fish, unless freshly caught, and meat have a strong smell, burden the air while being cooked, and leave a residue of unpleasant odors long after they have been consumed.

In Japan, China, and India, Westerners are avoided by the natives and snarled at by their dogs because heavy meat eating makes us smell funny. The same thing happens in the confines of a small boat. Since we cannot escape each other, and since others aboard may well be vegetarians, it is best to avoid abusing shipmates by renouncing meat altogether. Finally, the higher the protein content of food, the more complex are the digestive processes needed to convert it to energy and, since you are already confronted by the rolling and the roiling of the sea, it is best to tax your belly less rather than more.

Eating And Other Natural Functions

Let us direct our attention to the no-no's. What you do not in-gurgitate is as important as what you do. The manner in which you deal with the mechanics of eating—when and how much, as well as the related processes of evacuation and regurgitation—is as relevant as what goes into you. Here are some thoughts on foods and processes to avoid:

Avoid overeating. Leave food on your plate purposely and with forethought. This is an effective, but not often recommended, method of keeping seasickness at bay. A bloated tummy will be more attuned to nausea than one just pleasantly half full.

Avoid not eating. Even when a bit queasy you must get something down. Keeping a little food in you is the beginning of a sea change and an end to seasickness. Avoid abusing your digestive system by either too much or too little. The name of the nautical game is moderation in food as well as in all things.

Avoid dehydration. Drink lots and lots of water. You will need it. On one recent passage down the Red Sea each of us consumed between eight and ten liters of fluids a day. Most was sweated out long before it reached the kidneys. Drink lots of canned, unsweetened, fruit juices when your fresh fruit runs out. Be careful if your rioting sea tummy is one that generates excess acid, and be careful of those acidic juices. The best beverage, and cheapest, is water.

Avoid the sin of eating before lying down like you would avoid the plague. Your bunk is for sleeping. Digestion on a small boat is best accomplished in a more or less vertical position.

Avoid pastry. There is no excuse for cake. It is hard to digest, fattening and expensive. Yet a handful of plain cookies with coffee or tea on a night watch is a favorite pick-me up on most cruising boats.

No tobacco. No dope. The sea is exciting enough. Tobacco and drugs are born of the boredoms of land. Take a couple of deep breaths. At sea they will bend your mind as much as any hallucinogenic.

If you have to throw up do not fight it. If you get a signal to whoops then let it go (to lee, always to lee!). Throwing up, an apt term, is nature's automatic feedback. Your belly knows better than your head when it is beleaguered, so when you get the urge to feed the fish, do not resist. You will lose that battle anyway and be sicker for the delay.

When the sea is up and things are a bit hairy, going to the head seems like just too damn much trouble. Take the trouble! Never, never resist an anal urge. If you do you will only get a headache, or worse, as punishment. When I went into the army my Dad's advice was, "Keep your mouth shut and your bowels open." Most excellent advice for surviving a war and a long passage.

Perhaps these nine no-no's seem unimportant. Perhaps these matters are too marginal compared to the big things that worry you, like navigating and sail handling. But just try to navigate when constipated or handle sails when seasick. First things first; look to the small problems and the big stuff will work itself out.

Sailorly Foods

Sailorly foods do not discomfort your belly or your nose, and are low-energy foods that help control your waistline. They are foods that resist corruption and remain edible without refrigeration. They are, in a word, the preferred victuals of vegetarians.

They will stay fresh, are simple to cook, and generate only mild fragrances both in the cooking and in the eating. Sea-sensitized noses do not require the odoriferous concoctions of *nouvelle cuisine*. The sea brings us back to gustatory basics where even the most common foods taste good. An unexpected blessing.

PASTA

Pasta is the perfect sea food. Nothing is easier to keep or easier to cook. No food can be so endlessly varied as to appear a new dish for as many days and weeks you spend at sea. Everybody likes pasta.

RICE

The staple of the world, rice is cheap and available anywhere. It is accepting of endless sauces, keeps forever, and never smells up the galley. Rice serves equally well as a main course or as a side dish. Its disguises are as varied and as delicious as Pacific sunsets. A diet of rice with a piece of fruit, an occasional veggie, and some beans now and then is all the food that your body needs for a 30-day passage. Any more would be gilding the lily. Nice but not necessary.

GRAINS

All grains are sailorly. Hot cereal, cold cereal *sans* sugar coatings and *sans* raisins, and especially popcorn for a treat, will sit well and nourish sufficiently. Oats and barley and wheat, all good things to eat.

BEANS AND LEGUMES

Dried beans and legumes come back to life easily with a bit of water. They never go bad, take little space, and a variety are available everywhere. Beans and legumes are the major source of necessary protein that can replace abusive proteins of meat. Ignore the myth that beans make gas. They do no more than other stuff, and even if they should, you have a thousand miles to lee to flatuate toward.

EGGS

Contrary to opinion, eggs last for months without refrigeration. They are cheap and universally available, and what you cannot do to an egg you cannot do to food. But approach with caution. Eggs are a high-energy, high-protein food, and are a devil to digest. Egg yolks are an intense source of cholesterol. When you use eggs, try throwing half the yolk away. This will not affect the taste much and disabuses your arteries.

MILK

Milk is one of the foods that, when denatured by dessication, loses little of its appeal. The new high-temperature sterilized milk, in those tough little cardboard boxes, will outlast any passage and tastes remarkably like a milkman's delivery.

FRUIT

If the sea denies the sailor anything, it is a fresh piece of fruit. Denial of fresh fruit at sea reeducates us to the serendipity of seasonal fruit. On land, where oranges are flown from Jaffa, and grapes from the valleys of California arrive everyday, we have lost the wonder of fruit in season. The very best piece of fruit I ever had was a simple orange in the Galápagos after only ten days at sea. Its flavor burst in my mouth like a new idea. I will never forget that orange.

Some fresh fruit can be carried. A stalk of bananas will last more than long enough and a basket of tough little limes will still be around when you drop your hook in Papeete.

VEGGIES

Most will not last, but onions, the noblest of the vegetable kingdom, only need a bit of ventilation to continue to tickle your palate. Potatoes, too, and since it would be nice to have some green vegetables, the lowly cabbage will serve and serve and serve. Try spoiling a cabbage. Almost impossible. They do smell a bit but severe undercooking helps.

ONE AND ONE EQUALS THREE

The *combinations* of sailorly foods lead to good nutrition. Rice and beans eaten together will elegantly supply the necessary balance between protein, fat (of which you need only nano-amounts), and starch. Any nutritionist should be able to balance your list of sailorly foods in ten minutes.

Follow these guidelines and you will debark after a month at sea healthier, skinnier, and more pleased with yourself than you were ever before.

A few notes on food costs and preservation. In this world in which transport is easy and distances destroyed, any food that can be made to keep—either dried, frozen, or in a can— is likely to be available whatever outlandish harbor you sail into. Preservable foods abroad will cost almost the exact dollar price they will at home. A can of food will cost about the same in Sudan or Sri Lanka as it will in the supermarkets of home. Of course things may *seem* either cheaper or more expensive because of the different costs of other items. When you compare the cans, dollar for dollar, the only logical reason for heavily stocking up before you leave is that, while the prices will be the same abroad, the selection will not. What you get in Djibouti will cost the same as in Dearborn. You will simply not get, at any price, most of the stuff that loads the shelves in the U.S.

Fresh foods are the real bargains in foreign lands. The local markets are full of cheap and delicious fruits and vegetables. Although the variety is limited and very seasonal, and the foods will not keep very well, for a pittance you can eat fresh like a king in any Third World country. The best bargains are basics such as rice, wheat, and corn. Generally these staples are subsidized to the point of being, to you, almost cost-free.

The downside is that they have, or very quickly develop, creepy crawlies seemingly impossible to keep out. Nothing is impossible. Here is how to handle that problem.

One of the most ubiquitous products in the world is solid carbon-dioxide gas known in the U.S. as dry ice. It is cheap and plentiful, and when used as described here, it is the best preservative for dry solid foods that you can find.

Fill the bottoms of sealable wide-mouth plastic jugs (easily obtained) with a layer of dry ice. Cover with a sheet or two of paper and fill the container with rice or flour or corn. Screw on the cap loosely but do not seal. Let the dry ice evaporate. The heavier than air CO_2 displaces the air in the container leaving an atmosphere of pure CO_2. Then seal.

Nothing can live in an atmosphere of CO_2. Any creepies already in the food are immediately eliminated, and if they left eggs, their progeny perish as quickly as they are born. This will keep staples bug free for as long as any passage can last.

ESCAPE FROM SEXUAL EASE

Sex at sea isn't easy. There is altogether too much leaping about of the bunk to get much satisfaction. But the very lack of ease seems to add delectable dimensions to an act which, perhaps, has become a bit automatic on land. Sex at sea must be worked for and worked at. That's what makes it so special. Here are a few hints.

Who

There is no Mr. or Ms. Right at sea. There is only whoever there is. Your entire universe of choice has been reduced to one. Since you have no need to choose, and no distractions from greener grass, you have the precious opportunity to single-mindedly investigate your partner's hitherto unplumbed sexual depths.

What

Sex is not all copulation. Indeed sex at sea is not even mostly copulation. Coming in from a wet, cold, and scary watch to the sleeping invitation of a bunkmate's warm body can be ejaculative *sans* insertion. Unlike on land, there is no separation between what is and what is not sexual on a boat. Since you have time, opportunity, and the blessed absence of choice on a long passage, everything that happens between two people is sexual. What you do to each other and with each other in your otherwise unpeopled universe is not subject to society's shoulds and shouldn'ts. You are Adam and Eve (or Adam and Adam or Eve and Eve) in a watery garden presided over by gods more forgiving than Jehovah.

When

You might think that the endless contiguity of a small boat leads to sexual ennui. The truth is that there is damn little endless contiguity. You two meet infrequently in disposable time. Off watch moments are full of other things that must be done, chores that cannot be put off. The rare moments available for dalliance, the few odd hours off watch when you both are free and receptive, will be like lovers coming together after a long parting.

Where

In the rigging to the singing of the winds, in the engine room to the pound of the diesel, in the privacy of the foredeck, or tied to the mast in a storm, a small boat has so many more creative places to do it than do the repetitive restrictions of land. On land, sex becomes scheduled, and almost invariably happens in the bedroom. You do not really find many opportunities to screw, for example, on the hood of your car. Would you? At sea sex should and does serendipitously happen anywhere.

And How

Do not worry about how. Clothes are rarely an obstacle, a warm body is usually foreplay enough, and besides, your cavorting boat has a few new acrobatic tricks in store for you. But do, please, plan carefully for contraception. An unplanned pregnancy can be bothersome anywhere, but on a small boat on a long passage it can, like a collision at sea, ruin your entire day.

Sex and Odors

On land everybody worries about what they smell like. It is a wonder that we can breathe at all in the fog of deodorants, colognes, and perfumes that envelope us. There may be some small justification for this on land where everyone smells differently. But not at sea. At sea everyone smells equally good or bad. The odors of others, since they are the same as your own, go unnoticed. The Good Lord, who predated deodorants by a number of years, has arranged sexual things so that smells are part of the pleasures. Snort about a bit with your new, sea-cleansed nose, you are in for a pleasant, unpolluted surprise.

The clatter and clutter of land dulls us to all but the raucous of inputs. At sea the forgotten small delights of sex come roaring back into focus. A light touch, a warm bottom on a cold night, or the startle of a salty kiss lets you enter a sensory realm every bit as satisfactory as orgasm. Best of all is the rare opportunity to relearn the tender, relational depths of exclusivity. Never mind that we are true to each other only because there is no one else about. Never mind that choice has shrunk to just one body and mind. The fact remains that with too much choice, as on land, we more often than not never get to the erotic bottoms of just two people alone. The paradox is that escape from variety proves once again to be an escape into unimagined, unembarrassing riches.

If you ever found yourself in a jet at 30,000 feet, with a willing lady and no place to do it, you share with the cruising sailors of the world an ultimate frustration. There are a number of places in which the barriers to coupling are so forbidding that it can only be accomplished in extremis. But the human condition being what it is, whatever the barriers, they are sooner or later overcome.

Let us consider some of the more arcane locales or conditions in which the passage of seed has been accomplished. For teenagers, the back seats of cars are relatively comfortable and accessible. In the days of the American monster autos there was a certain amount of comfort and even elegance in doing your date in the back seat, even though the couple you doubled with had carefully adjusted the rear view mirror to view the action.

With the shrinking of autos, comfort and elegance have disappeared.

A car is essentially a public place which, for some, may have been an added spice. Public coupling is a common, if dangerous, practice in all of the world, especially in Israel. The complaint in Israel is that if you "screw in the street, everyone will stop and give you advice."

Splintery knot holes and barbed wire (ugh!) fences have failed to deter incarcerers from having it off with incarcerees. There are moments and places when the completion of the act presents such clear and present dangers that one wonders at the inattention to safety and survival of the celebrants. There is the tale, perhaps apocryphal but no less apropos, of the couple who chose railroad tracks and failed to disentangle as a train roared into view. The train screeched to a stop just inches from the energetic pair. A furious engineer dismounted and loudly remonstrated to the couple who by this time had done the deed and were adjusting their clothing. Rather than being disconcerted by the loud attack, the man on the tracks quietly pointed out to the engineer that, "You were coming, I was coming, she was coming, and you were the only one with brakes." The engineer thought about this for a moment and, being a reasonable man, quietly remounted his train and chugged off.

For most of us, deviants aside, intercourse is an intensely private confrontation that requires a reasonably comfortable platform or position and a temperature that neither fries nor freezes. While most of the time a contortion can be found that will result in insertion, the more arcane the twisting the more stable must be the platform in order to prevent serious injury. If you are going to do it in a phone booth then the booth must be at least firmly planted in the ground and the glass not too frangible. If in an auto, it is far better parked than bumping along a rutted back road. Even in a bed, the connection between headboard and springs should be secure lest lusty heroics separate them and land you in a discouraging heap on the floor.

I have never been a fan of water beds since they preclude getting a firm grip on anything. Feather beds, into which your love disappears in clouds of linen, can create entanglements that, tourniquet like, cut off the blood supply to arms, legs, and other important appendages. Personally, feathers make me sneeze.

Privacy, warmth, and stability are required for the arena of love. The arena itself must have enough space to swing your sexual cat and should be fixtured in such a manner as to encourage the often exhausting and sometimes ludicrous comings together, if that immortal condition can ever be accomplished at all.

But to get back to sailing, can you think of a less likely place than a small sailboat asea that fits the minimum requirements for successful sex? I cannot. There is simply no privacy. In addition to a lack of space, a sailboat below is nothing more than a boom box, an echo chamber in which the slightest sigh of delight becomes an announcement to the crew that you are doing it. The need to suppress the small, and sometimes not so small, gurgles, chortles, splutters, and synchrony of sex is enough to make you forgo the whole process to begin with.

If you cannot at some epiphanic moment be allowed a long and loud "Yessss," or even an adulatory and thankful "Oh God," much of the pleasure is painfully swallowed like a sneeze unemitted. And how about all those small, but vital directions such as, put that here, or open those, or ooh that tickles, or even watch it you're breaking my arm. How in creation, which this obviously is not, can you avoid decent, or more to the point, indecent instructions without the entire crew picturing, imperfectly, the activity that is going on? What in the world, they will wonder to themselves later as you meet on watch, what in the world was he doing with his arm there? Actually they will not really know where "there" is but the wonder will never cease.

If you have ever screwed on a sailboat you will already know that, privacy aside, there just is no reasonably satisfactory place to do it. Sea berths are properly designed to compact the sailor into a face-up, horizontal position in which both sides, the top of his head, and the soles of his feet, are tightly braced against motion. A really good sea berth is not at all dissimilar to a coffin, except that a coffin is somewhat more roomy and much more softly upholstered.

Lee boards further limit the sailor from achieving a giving/receiving position and raise the problem of, "How the hell are we going to get your legs open?" At some point the problems become so acute that either you or both of you descend into paroxysms of uncontrollable laughter, further puzzling your crewmates, or simply give up in disgust.

Should you seek a wider arena aboard, you find that there is nothing any better than your bunk below. Topsides, on deck, what space is not crowded with dinghies, spare fuel, and unstowed sails is cold, wet, and slippery. Should you come to terms with the cold and wet, it becomes necessary to don a safety belt. Think about that for a moment.

The lack of privacy, absent an amenable temperature and simple paucity of places to do it, is nothing compared to the ultimate insult that a sailboat inflicts on all activities, not only sexual ones. However, the damage done by this final insult is most egregious when applied to the gentle and loving act of procreation.

The final insult is movement, the endless, unanticipatable thrust and parry of a sailboat in a seaway, any seaway. Beyond the nausea and the thousand and one other symptoms that emerge from the motion of a sailboat, there is still another more real, more physical, interdiction. That is the lurching and the upping and downing and the siding to siding that are never consonantal, let alone conducive, with the measured and succulent inning and outing of successful sexual comity.

The motion of the surface of the sea attacks the rhythm of sex, the very drumbeat of procreation, to which our hormones prance their exquisite gavotte. When you are managing your partner and managing yourself and keeping both from being bodily erupted onto the deck, how in the world can you be expected to manage your orgasm and have some little bit of concern left over for hers?

One of the great recreational untruths in the world is that romantic fol-de-rol that sailing encourages coupling and cohabitation. The charter people should know better. Indeed, they do know better since they do their own osculatory (and more) activities back at their comfortable and unmoving offices. But the seed is sown, if not in vaginas then in the heads of sailors yearning for the thrust of bowsprits into combing seas along with the accompanying romantic thrusts. Sailors are convinced that sailing is sexy. They believe that what does not happen easily at home in bed will soar to new heights on a boat. The only thing that is likely to soar is you out of your bunk.

In spite of all evidence to the contrary, the belief that sailing is sexy is on par with the statement that the Aegean is fun to sail in. Both are harmful to your health. And heaven forfend that you expose, as you will, your pallid dermis to an arrogant sun and receive, as you will, a burn that penetrates to your very soul. And then some oaf, perhaps a mite less scorched, appears above you sandpapering your redness with unwanted attention. Under these circumstances the withholding of conjugal favors is the most mild reaction, impalement on a safety stanchion may be the most extreme and I daresay you could convince a judge of mitigation. Especially if the judge is a sailor.

The truth is that, in spite of difficulties, sailors are a lusty folk. The most common story about sailors is that they have a girl in every port. Is it any wonder that they have a girl in every port since that seems to be the only possible way that they can get any? Sailors are as powerfully horny on land as they are powerfully deprived at sea.

Sailor, if you want to screw, stay home. If you want to conjoin with the universe, a rather larger matter than with your mate, then by all means take to the world of the sea. You have a clear choice, sex or serendipity, there is no best of both worlds at sea.

Of course, you do eventually reach land.

RELEARNING THE JOYS OF SLEEP

Sleep on land is pale and wanting compared to sleep on a small sailboat. We earn our sleep on a sailboat and it comes readily into our arms. Rather than wooing it more or less unrequitedly as we must do amidst the ease and sloth of our landbound lives, sleep slams into us at any moment that we find ourselves free of the endless tasks of sail.

In seeking sleep on land we form our bedrooms into temples of Somnus. We suppress the light, banish sound, and soften mattresses into cloudlike billows. We make "white noise" and wear sleep masks and take warm milk and alcohol and finally the damned pills that put us into a sleep from which we only half awake the next day. We fight desperately for that healing release that should be ours by right but nightly escapes us.

But ship out on a sailboat on a blue-water passage and from the first night you will be fighting not to sleep, fighting to keep your weary self awake. Nothing interferes. Neither lights in your face nor the rushing noises of passage in your ears have the strength to pierce sleep's shell at sea.

There is one thing, however, that must be attended to lest, like Hamlet's complaint, it "doth murder sleep." A damp bunk is bearable, indeed you can accustom yourself to wet and gritty linen. But no one can bear the insidious drip of cold water from an insistent leak from above. The banishment of leaks over bunks must be among the first order of a skipper's business. Almost nothing is as important.

Some Thoughts on Sleep

A BUNK IS THE SAILOR'S CASTLE

If it can be arranged, do not "hot bunk." There should be at least one absolutely private space on a small and crowded vessel, a bed untrammeled by others. The sailor's bunk should be available at any time for a snooze or a nap or a bit of horizontal dreaming. To be made to stand in line for a bed is unconscionable.

DRY

The daily airing of linen and the incredible surprise of changed sheets every few days rate four stars in any marine Michelin.

SHEETS

Fitted, lightweight flannel sheets are the stuff that make life worthwhile. Unfitted sheets bunch up and quickly escape from the careful tucking to which you subjected them. If you want to know how to fit any sheet to any bunk simply look at how an ironing-board cover is cinched tight to the board. Do the very same to your sheets.

BIGGER ISN'T BETTER

Small is best. The less room to roam about in, or be thrown about in, the better. Say no to double beds. These vast surfaces are designed for motels with mirrored ceilings, air conditioning, and rooms that do not move. They are not for a sailboat where two in a large bed is anti-social, anti-sleep, and anti-erotic.

HARD/SOFT

Billows of hard pillows to jam between hard bulkheads and soft bodies are *de rigueur*. However, the mattresses should be hard and totally unsprung. The surge and sink that springs will subject you to on a sailing vessel make me nauseous even to write about.

CURTAINS

We are all more or less ashamed of what we do in bed even though we learn on a small boat that everyone else is also subject to the sinful cringing we suffer from in our secret lives. I see no reason why the hardships of a passage on a small boat should eliminate the last small, solitary piece of personal comfort to which some of us own up, and to which all of us are habituated. An ocean passage abuses us sufficiently in less pleasant ways than we might abuse ourselves.

The fiction, if not the fact, of privacy can be accomplished by a yard of cloth. Then if you do whatever you do quietly, behind a curtain, you can foolishly imagine that you are getting away with something.

LIGHTING

Your bunk is where you will read. Provide small, shaded, directable lights. Fifteen watts is too much.

WARMTH

Even in the tropics it gets chilly at night. For these cool evenings a very light *cotton* blanket is best, preferably one with a loose and open weave. It is called a thermal blanket and, sandwiched between two sheets, it lightly and effectively holds in the heat. As close as 15° from the equator it can get damn cold, so some wool should be kept aboard.

BUNKBOARDS

De rigueur! Heavy, no nonsense, wooden bunkboards are best. Something you can throw all your weight against without fear of flying out of your bunk. Make very sure that, as they bend a bit under your weight, the fastenings to the ends of the bunk are secure.

BANISH THE SUN FROM BELOWDECKS

Much sleeping will be done offwatch in daylight hours. The sun, especially the tropical sun, sneaks below through the tiniest openings and burns into closed eyes and deep sleep like a laser. While the sun climbs and sets and the boat wanders and lurches, the sunbeam angles can get pretty weird. Ban the sun. A dancing, slashing, white-hot spear of sunlight can murder sleep as effectively as a slow salt water leak.

DECENT EXPOSURE

If you already know everything there is to know about the inside of your shipmates' heads, then the outsides of their bodies are no big deal. The escape from drape is natural on a small vessel among good friends. The sharing of nakedness teaches that we are really all pretty much the same. The horror of nudity is based not in guilt but in ego. We are *all* convinced that we are ugly, and hiding our bodies makes us somehow less objectionable. When we come to the sea and see that our shipmates are as funny looking—and as beautiful—as we ourselves are, clothes go overboard with ego. What a relief!

One of the obvious advantages of nakedness is that your skin washes clean more easily than any clothing. No matter how dirty you are you will always smell better than the clothes you take off. So, when you go into the bilge, go in naked. You will move more slowly (a good thing) so as to avoid the sharp places and the hot spots and when you emerge looking like a London chimney sweep, get a shipmate to sluice you down with a bucket. Sluicing is fun. It is much like showering with a friend and often leads to massage.

The obvious disadvantage of nakedness is exposure to the brutality of the burning sun.

The Pareo—All the Covering You Will Ever Need

There are times when some covering will be needed. Perhaps a ship lifts over the horizon, or the sun is too hot, or the evening breezes carry a chill. At these times the pareo is the universal answer and serves equally well for men and women.

To fashion a pareo, get a meter of light cotton cloth two meters wide. That's it. That's all the instruction you need to create a garment that will cover, hide, protect, and even act as a towel *après* sluicing. It can be rinsed clean in a cup of precious sweet water and after an hour in the sun, either on you or hanging from the rigging, it will smell as fresh as the claims of a detergent ad. When you go ashore, formally dressed in old shorts, your pareo will become the sack for the food you carry back from the marketplace.

A Wardrobe for Going Ashore

There might be times when the locals invite you to dinner. For the men, a pair of jeans and a short-sleeved open shirt is universally acceptable. Women are expected to dress up a bit, in something a little exotic. The more *outré* the creations, salted with a bit of *audace*, the better.

When You Are Invited to the Ambassador's Formal Dinner

Forget it, you won't be. And if you are invited, don't go. They are deadly dull. Go nowhere near where a tie is required.

The Sun, the Wonderful, Awful Sun

Notwithstanding the obvious joys of déshabillé, you must protect yourself from the wonderful, awful sun. The amount of clothing, or the lack of it, must be a function of latitude and time of day. The nearer you are to the equator and the nearer to noon, the more you will need to protect yourself from being fried.

One out of a hundred Americans will develop skin cancer. The more sun the more cancer. The proper use of clothing is to hide your body, not from the concupiscent glances of shipmates, which, in truth, do you little damage, but from the havoc that the sun visits on the unprotected light skins of the north. A tan looks wonderful, feels great, and invites stroking. But the cancer it invites isn't worth the candlepower.

Sunburn, like radioactive burn, is cumulative and permanent. A dermatologist recently studied the deep epidermal levels of the backsides and the faces of a ten-year old and a seventy-year old. He found that the backside skin of both, protected from the sun since birth, showed little difference or deterioration, whereas the facial skin of the seventy-year old recorded decades of attack from the sun. Years do not age your skin, the sun does. Every dollop of sun leaves a residue of age. A sunburn is never cured, the redness and the pain go away, but the deep damage accumulates.

Black, brown, tan and yellow skins have sunscreens built in. But if you are descended from the wan peoples of the north then you must, especially on a boat, develop sensible and protective ways of enjoying the sun.

From the hours of 11 A.M. to 3 P.M. in low latitudes your skin should be protected either by clothes or sun block.

Sun blocks are available in various numbered strengths. An ointment labeled ten will allow as much sun through in ten hours as would be absorbed in one hour without it. For our purposes, the higher the number the better. Remember that perspiration washes off most sun block. Reapply frequently. The newer blocks are grease based, waterproof, and are applied like lipstick.

Since your face takes most of the abuse, a broad brimmed hat and sun block should be worn from early in the morning till late afternoon. Protect your lips too.

That great promontory, your nose, is the most horizontal part of your face and thus gathers in more high-angle, noonday sun than any other part of you. Be nice to your nose. Send it flowers, give it nice smells, and lots and lots of Number 30 block.

Be as wary on cloudy as on sunny days. The burning rays slide through clouds as if they were not there. You may feel cool on cloudy days but your skin will fry.

Burning rays are reflected upward from sea and deck surfaces, so even a hat will not protect you entirely. During the really hot hours go below.

For eye protection, most ophthalmologists recommend wrap-around sunglasses with UV protection. Buy top quality. Don't forget a safety strap, especially if you wear prescription glasses.

The best sunglasses in the world for me are no more than little plastic cups into which a slit has been cut. The cups fit tightly against the eye, thus banning any sunlight sneaking in from the sides. The slit mechanically reduces all light, both visible and invisible, and allows the iris to then determine how much light the eye wants without reducing acuity at all. While offering great protection, these glasses do reduce your field of vision and should be reserved for leisure time.

Not Too Shoddy

The best footwear aboard is no footwear. There was never devised a shoe that will give a better grip on a deck than a naked foot. Shoeless sailors develop wonderful calluses on the soles of their feet, where calluses belong and not, as a result of shoddy shodding, on their tender tootsies. Bare feet on board is the rule with the exception of working the foredeck, especially at night in heavy weather.

Never, never, go about in socks unless you enjoy bouncing off the hard parts of your deck. Socked feet slip. Tuck socks away. Better yet, deep-six all socks. The all-time best reason for going shoeless is that deck shoes smell to high heaven and feet don't.

CHAPTER **5**

Safety

THE SEA KEEP

A boat is little more than a cave in which your exhausted tribe is huddled, escaping the terrors of shrieking winds and invisible seas. For those few hours, when you accept their lives and safety into your hands, there stands nothing between them and disaster save unwavering attention to inviolable duty. Watchkeeping, deep in our collective memories, is a core activity of any off-shore passage.

A good watchkeeping plan is your first defense against disaster at sea. The care with which a watchkeeping system is designed bears directly on its ability to function. If the skipper has not weighed and measured the human material he is dealing with in so elementary a matter as watchkeeping, then the passage itself bodes ill.

All watch plans seem concerned with developing a system in which the "dead hand of routine" is relieved by hopscotching each crew's watch around the clock. I do not think that hop-scotching is a very good idea. I am very fond of the dead hand of routine, and I am convinced that crew—and all the rest of us—comes to love what it knows best and hates even the hint of change. My own approach is to set fixed watch hours and fixed crew assignments to those hours.

To become a sailor you must have enough background to separate crisis from event, and that comes only after the sea has had the opportunity to test you a hundred times. The crises of 3 A.M. do not all appear within the hours of a single watch. They will appear and have to be dealt with in the course of a month, or perhaps a year, of watches. That is how sailors are made. It is like tying a bowline. Do it over and over again till the knot thunks quietly into place. Once you have conquered one knot go on to the next. Once you have conquered one watch, with all of its subtleties, go on to the next.

Fixed hours and fixed watches need not preclude consideration for individual preferences. However much the skipper tries to tailor boat needs to crew preferences, it is likely that not all will be pleased with their assignment. Offers of trades, even though both parties agree, must be quashed lest they violate the thoughtful pattern of watch allocations (soon to be discussed) that the skipper must go through.

The first consideration is the number of hours of watch. On a boat of 40 feet, on an offshore passage where 24-hour watches *must* be kept, the most congenial and peaceful pattern is "three on and nine off." This limits the watches, especially those kept at night, to a length during which there can be no excuse for nodding off. Everyone has a day watch and a night watch, nine full and delicious hours of leisure uninterrupted save by chores. It also gives everyone the opportunity to repetitively experience the watchkeeping needs of both the light and the dark hours.

Six out of 24 hours of full and alert duty at the wheel are as much as a cautious captain can expect of *quality* watchkeeping. Those of you who have not yet been at sea on a small boat at night may not appreciate how fierce the struggle to remain awake can be. Everything conspires toward sleep. The emptiness of the space about you, the sonority and the rhythms of the sea, and the damp chill that comes at night found even in the lowest latitudes, all whisper "sleep," especially at the end of the second hour of a three-hour watch.

When and by whom watches are kept is subject to one immutable precondition. The skipper's watch always occurs during the twilight hours at dawn and dusk. These are the navigational and the meteorological hours during which the sextant is unboxed and sights are taken. These magic, prescient hours of just-before-darkness and just-before-dawn are the times when a weatherwise skipper can see the shape of his next day in the sky.

While the skipper's watch establishes the selection process, the rest of the watchkeeps are parceled out on a curious question of personality. The moment of relief, a marvelously apt word, is the moment upon which much of the peace of the passage depends. Should a relieving watch be a minute late disaster portends, a minute early and all will go well. Whether an individual watchkeeper comes on duty early or late is more a matter of personality than of sloth or laziness. A crewmember who always shows up 15 minutes early will, curiously enough, rarely worry about relief being 15 minutes late. The crew who always is 15 minutes late will tear the heart out of a relief who has the audacity to take one extra minute. This is an immutable law of the sea.

The gales you will meet at sea may not be manipulated, but the emotional storms of the crew, no less dangerous, no less destructive of the comity of the voyage, lie within the range of calming options open to a thoughtful skipper. The moment of relief is more than just a changing of keepers. It involves passing along, between two sleepy, perhaps seasick, and certainly bemused people, all technical information concerning where the boat has been, how all of the systems have behaved, and toward where the boat should be headed in the next three hours. A timely relief allows for an unimpassioned transfer of authority in which all seamanly matters can be dealt with between friends rather than between impatient opponents. This is the moment when the outgoing watch passes along all learned in the past three hours so that the relieving watch may benefit by this experience. The real learning process at sea is as intimate, and as petty, as this.

Two out of every four sailors will generally be early and forgiving, and two will be late and unaccommodating. The trick is not to waste the two earlybirds on each other. The skipper must study the relieving habits of his crew carefully and reshuffle assignments to assure that there is peace at the relieving moments.

On long passages in a small boat one watchkeeper is usually sufficient. This is especially true if autopilots and wind vanes are present, and I don't know of anyone who chooses to sail without one or the other. The watchkeeper, when alone day or night, must *always* wear a safety harness when out of the cockpit on deck. An exception to "one at watch" could be a loving couple who ask for six hours of privacy in the cockpit under the cloak of the night. By all means, Skipper, encourage this sort of activity. If an amorous interlude can be created, well, why not? There is certainly the possibility of danger arising during those transcendent moments, but I will not accept that the universe is so accidental that it would be in precisely those few moments that a great tanker would loom and threaten.

There are endless things that can go bang in the night when your boat is under sail with a bone in her teeth. As safe as she may be, the bangs will more likely happen in darkness when you cannot see them coming and avoid them. A sail will blow out from a bit of chafe, or from a small tear that might have been seen and attended to in daylight. An engine, beginning to complain a bit, has a better chance of being heard by eight ears spread around the boat, topside and inside, than by the two ears of a keeper huddled against the cold far astern in the cockpit. A cycling pressure waterpump that can siphon off all of your precious water in a few short hours is almost impossible to hear except from below.

Since the list of possible debacles stretches out frighteningly, it becomes necessary to do more than just "stand" watch. On an offshore passage the watch must be "kept" and the keeper must be constantly on the prowl. The deck must be circumnavigated regularly in search of potential problems, the cockpit investigated, lines tested, and the steering worried over, all in a regular routine. Now and then the night watchkeeper must slip quietly below, with a well-shielded flashlight, to check the integrity of the hull. The keeper must peer in the bilges, check the stove shutoff valves, and make sure that neither rain nor sea is disturbing the sleep of his mates.

Night watch may also be small repair time, although concentrating on chores can make it too easy to forget the primary reason for being up and about. The watchkeeper is "up and about" (I love that phrase because it is precisely what a keeper should be doing) primarily to prevent the boat from bumping into another boat or a cute little rock. The integrity of your hull is more likely to be explosively violated by something hard from without than by a teredo worm or a loose hose clamp from within. And never forget it.

There were three of us on our Westsail 32 making a transatlantic passage from Dakar in Senegal to the U.S. We had passed the bleak Cape Verde Islands and were settling in for the long and lovely tradewind passage ahead of us. Since we were only three aboard, the watches were longer than I would have liked. Night watches were still kept to three hours and we added hours in the daylight.

Of the three, Marilyn was on her very first ocean passage. Rolf, Swedish born, was an experienced sailor and, as a Westsail dealer, was invaluable to have aboard.

The problem that beset us centered around the fact that Rolf had just turned 45 and had been prescribed his first pair of eyeglasses. He was sensitive to them and was convinced that any small speck would interfere with his vision. On the night watch in question, Rolf checked the horizon, declared it clear of shipping, and came below to clean his glasses. While below he poured himself a cup of coffee and headed back topsides. He had been below at most ten minutes.

As he popped his head out of the companionway hatch we heard a loud Swedish equivalent of "Oh my God!" Marilyn and I rushed on deck in time to watch an endless wall of steel that blocked out the sky and seemingly stretched from horizon to horizon. A huge super tanker whipping along at what seemed like 30 knots in the calm sea had come up and was passing us not ten yards away. Her bow wave set our small vessel almost on beam ends. We watched in terror as the mast just missed the wall of steel as she rushed passed. As she sailed blithely and unknowingly away, the turbulence from her great screw wrenched us about, dumping supplies all over the cabins, and almost hurling the three of us overboard.

The mast and the sails survived and luckily so since the shaking up we received fouled our oil lines and our injectors. We could no longer use our diesel and had to finish the remaining 2000 miles under sail.

A hairsbreadth more and there would have been another mysterious disappearance since the big tanker never did see us. But it was not the big tanker's fault. We were guilty of the most egregious error that a small boat can suffer. We had failed in our watchkeeping.

Failed by only ten minutes . . . but that was more than enough to invite disaster.

It can never be said too many times that, at sea level, your horizon is only three miles away. Make that five miles to allow for the mast height of the light coming over the horizon, although a tenet of navigational safety at sea is to *always* assume that you are closer to anything you might bump into rather than farther away. In light of this assumption, it also bears endless repetition that big ships rarely do less than 20 knots. Twenty knots means they will cover the five miles from your horizon in 15 minutes, which is about the time it takes to get a cup of soup, move a bowel, or glance through an old magazine. The prudent skipper and the intelligent crew will ever be aware that a collision at sea, an utter, complete, and total disaster by any reckoning, is only 15 minutes away at any time during your entire passage. That is your margin. Fifteen minutes on your back, musing at the stars, may be the last stars at which you will ever muse.

But as real as the danger is, the watchkeeper can easily "pop and swivel" the danger away. Whatever you are doing you must "pop" up and make a 360° "swivel" to survey the little universe of which your boat is the center. A good sailor can always be identified by these two strange motions of pop and swivel. Should you be ashore in some little bistro and notice that the guy at the end of the bar who smells a bit musty and who has had his face in his beer for 15 minutes suddenly pops up and swivels about to check out the action, you may safely sign him on. He will give great watch.

One last word on watchkeeping. Since the skipper has accepted the final and total responsibility for all souls aboard, it is the skipper's fate to be awakened at night. You must train the crew to have no pity, and to rust you out at the slightest sign of anything at all changing on or near the boat. No matter how capable, a watchkeeper does not and cannot bear the ultimate burden of responsibility. Responsibility is the skipper's shtick. Responsibility is nontransferable. The *first* obligation that a watch has is to share everything with the skipper.

Violation of this obligation, out of concern for the skipper's sleep or for whatever reason, occurs all too often, and frequently with the skipper's quiet acceptance. Alas, even at sea we are in danger of becoming too permissive a society.

HEAVY WEATHER AVOIDANCE

The central purpose of this book is to motivate first-time offshore passagemaking. For those who may have little experience and large fears about the sea, we suggest that they are not likely to test themselves too severely the first time out. Knowing how to handle a small boat in really awful weather is a skill acquired by very few sailors because there is so little really awful weather out there, and it can usually be avoided. A reasonably cautious sailor might sail for a lifetime before getting the opportunity to test out a strong gale.

A really awful storm is really awful. It attacks you on all fronts; it makes you sick; it shatters your eardrums; it exhausts you physically; and it destroys any emotional equanimity you may have acquired. It damages your image of yourself as a human being and as a sailor, and if all that were not enough, a bad storm has a good chance of killing you.

To deal with all this you must play the storm game. The storm game is called Avoidance, a game remarkably easy to play. The big storms, the hurricanes and the North Atlantic gales, appear in narrow and defined windows of geography and time and a sailor would have to be astoundingly unlucky or fantastically foolish to find his anemometer pinned at 90 knots.

Heavy Weather Avoidance in the Atlantic

All you need to know about surviving an ultimate storm in the Atlantic is that you must not get caught in one. All of the non-ultimate storms that you will experience in the Atlantic, your boat will survive for you. Learn from her as you go to sea. She is a good sailor. Should you fail to follow these instructions, experienced sailors will wash their hands of you, and the chances are that the sea will wash more of you than that. Even the finest sailors in the most seaworthy boats who choose, from hubris, to test themselves against bad weather, survive North Atlantic gales and Atlantic hurricanes by mostly sheer good luck.

Follow these two simple rules and the beginner will never again need to fear the Atlantic Ocean.

Rule: Cross the central North Atlantic only in June.

Rule: Avoid the Caribbean and Atlantic during hurricane season.

In sensible sailing seasons the chance of running into anything over 30 knots in the Atlantic is as rare as dry socks. Stay below 35° N in the eastern North Atlantic between the beginning of December and the end of June and the probability of running into any wind above 30 knots is almost nil. Should you venture above 35°, the chances for gales and storms increase. Do not go there.

Heavy Weather Avoidance in the Pacific

For the Pacific there is only one rule, which should not be hard to remember and will give you plenty of room to wander about.

Rule: Do not sail north of Hawaii at any time, or west of Tahiti during typhoon season.

North of Hawaii one begins to get high latitude weather and not too far west of Tahiti the great typhoon systems begin. Monsoons you can weather, typhoons you cannot. Since the season for typhoons is long and their appearances and routes are unpredictable, it would be sensible for the beginner sailor to dally in Tahiti till a weather window opens. Not a bad place for dalliance.

The appearances of typhoons have a rhythm, and typhoon forecasters have them about half figured out. The good news is that you will get about five days warning that a storm *could* hit you. The bad news is that the forecasters are as yet unable to absolutely predict whether it will or not.

The Other Oceans

Even a quick perusal of sailing and pilot charts will enable you to form your own rules about the other oceans of the world. In all of the places that you will want to sail, there is always a safe window of time and place. Sometimes the window is very small and might require a bit of waiting about. Should you want to go safely and comfortably across the Indian Ocean from Aden to Sri Lanka you can only do so in September. You might have to muck about in the Mediterranean for a summer.

Heavy Weather Tactics

Should you want further information on heavy weather sailing, you need seek no further than Adlard Coles' *Heavy Weather Sailing*. He said it all and he said it first and no one has said anything as important about heavy weather since. Coles will take you through the available tactics in case the sea tries to do you in. Which tactic you actually choose in the actual event depends more on the circumstances of the storm than on your preference.

Avoidance of great storms is another case of accommodating yourself to the realities of the sea. You cannot beat the storms. Indeed you can barely survive the bad ones and not even always that. As in most matters between you and the sea, you must give in. Giving in to a storm is best done by escaping it beforehand. Remember that it is neither a great honor to survive an unnecessary storm nor a disgrace to avoid one.

ANCHORING SAFELY

Scope

The most important concept in safe anchoring is scope. Scope is simply the distance to anchor divided by depth of water under your keel. Scope is a ratio, not a linear measurement. You do not, as so many advise, "let out scope." You let out rode, and the more rode you let out the larger the ratio of scope you create. Generally speaking, the larger the ratio the more securely your boat will be fastened to the bottom. This is all you need to know. The single commandment of anchoring is, "Thou shalt create scope." All else is commentary.

CREATING SCOPE

The more rode that is let out, the longer the line is between boat and anchor, the more scope is created. This is a first principle to which there are no exceptions. If you are using chain, and you should use nothing else, the weight of the chain adds efficiency to the anchor. When a great deal of chain is paid out, it is likely that the anchor will never even feel the pull of the boat. The pull is completely absorbed by the heavy chain as it is lifted from the sea bed in response to the pull of the boat. The catenary—the curve that the chain assumes between your anchor and your boat—of the chain does not hold the boat; the weight of the chain as the boat attempts to lift it off the bottom both provides holding power long before the pull gets to the anchor, and provides shock absorption as the pull is absorbed, link by heavy link, while lifted from the bottom.

Whatever anchor you are using, the heavier the chain and the longer the chain, the more secure you will be, and the less pull the anchor will be called upon to hold. The ultimate discussion of anchor types, styles, and techniques depends on the weight of the rode and the amount of scope. Whatever style of anchor you choose, scope will improve its holding power.

When you understand this, the argument against line and in favor of chain for the main anchor is inescapable. Line provides none of the weight that eases the strain on the anchor and, in addition, is subject to chafe, which chain is not. Some argue that the advantage of nylon is that it stretches, and thus provides shock absorption. That very well may be, but at the point at which nylon is absorbing shock, it is also pulling hard at the anchor to create that stretch. The shock absorption induced by chain does not depend on pulling against the anchor. With line you pull against the set of the anchor. Nylon "works" an anchor, chain rarely does. With chain you are calling on the infinite forces of gravity long before the strain ever reaches the anchor. The steady unvarying pull of the chain tends to set the anchor ever more firmly.

Whatever the subtle little truths of the physics of anchor design might be, the overriding advantage lies in the weight of the chain. Pile on as much chain as your little vessel can handle. If the weight is too much, deep-six a generator, or something.

For those of you who might want to roam the exotic places of the Third World, nylon presents an additional problem. The value of a 100 feet or so of 3/4-inch nylon rode represents a good part of the average annual income of many places in the world. Anchored boats have often lost their nylon rode to the thief's knife, and have been left precariously dangling on a piece of rotten manila. It is not quite as easy to cut chain.

For those boats with bobstays, the rode presents a substantial problem. As the boat moves about on its tether, a nylon rode chafes quietly against the bobstay and will eventually part. While a chain will not chafe and therefore not part, it will make an awful noise all night long and, in truth, cannot be doing the bobstay much good. The solution is a "turtle," rarely used, and even more rarely described.

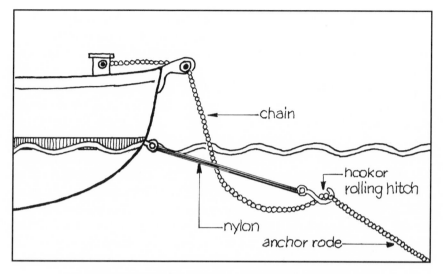

The Turtle: The Perfect Answer to Everything in Anchoring.

As you see from the diagram, the turtle, no more than a piece of nylon, accomplishes the following:

> *Since the turtle pulls* against the weight of the chain, it provides the stretch of nylon without directly pulling against the anchor.

> *By lowering the point* of attachment of the rode *below* the bobstay, it prevents the chafe of nylon and the deafening noise of chain.

> *By lowering the point* of attachment of the rode, it *increases the scope.* A much to be desired condition.

> *And, should things get really hairy* and should the turtle part, you will be alerted to the worsening conditions by being thrown out of your bunk when the boat is brought up against the chain. I really do not know why everybody does not use a turtle.

Note that you should attach the turtle to the rode with a slipped rolling hitch with a tail long enough to reach the deck. This allows you to free the rode from the deck for anchor retrieval.

Anchors

At the beginning of WWII the English found themselves in need of a really good anchor to hold the barges that they proposed to hurl across the English Channel at the Germans. The anchors then in use were variations of the classic fisherman's anchor, which had been used as long as sailors could remember. Upon testing this old tried-and-true design, they discovered that its holding power was less than they would need for a heavy barge in the chancy seas of the Channel.

The English were blessed with a collection of eccentric scientists called boffins. These "back room boys" came up with the anchor we know as the CQR. Starting with the concept of a plow, they so designed the blade that the harder it was pulled upon, the deeper it tried to dig itself in. The British, being nothing if not cute, chose these three letters to name their new anchor because if you say them quickly they come out "Secure," which indeed the new anchor proved to be. There is nothing available today, or indeed likely to be available for a very long time, that in my opinion comes as close to being as perfect as is the CQR. The only exception is the Danforth, which is about 25 percent less efficient, and which will skitter around like water on a hot griddle when you try to set it in grass. The Danforth, however, is superb in sand.

If you are anchored in a current that is likely to reverse itself and cause your boat to swing, use bow *and* stern anchors. And if you expect any kind of a blow, say 25 knots and upward, do not be shy about laying out two anchors from your bow.

THE LIFERAFT

At a recent boat show I inspected a six-person raft. It looked a bit flimsy and certainly too small for six. The dummy arranged inside the raft used up almost all of the floor space. I asked a salesman about the size, as it would have been impolite to challenge him on the raft's flimsiness, and he countered with the statement that this raft had been "selected by the U.S. Coast Guard as its official liferaft." I was impressed. But only for a moment. As I studied the raft I realized that, as a private offshore sailor, I was the last person for whom this raft was designed and equipped.

Liferaft design is a reflection of the military protocol that rescue must be accomplished in the first 72 hours. This leaves offshore passagemakers with a choice of emergency liferafts that are great for three days, barely adequate for a week, and a total disaster for any period longer than that. The experiences of those cast adrift in liferafts tell us that a raft should be designed for many months of hard use, without the necessity to expend limited energies on keeping the raft afloat.

Adapting Liferaft Systems

We must turn our attention to adapting and enhancing the existing design with devices and materials that will extend the raft's useful life, will provide sustenance while we are aboard, and will call loud attention to us in the presence of possible rescue.

These systems, in order of importance, are:

Water supply
Liferaft repair
Food supply
Signaling

Water Supply

This is the most important problem to be solved. If you do not have water, you will either be too weak or too dead to confront the other problems. Every report from survivors is full of concern for their water, and all tell of the enormous amount of time and work expended on assuring an adequate supply.

Canned Water. This is the least efficient way of providing water. Cans are heavy, bulky, potentially leaky, and you cannot carry more than a couple of days' supply. This reflects the military conviction that you should be given only three days or so to live. Retain canned water in your raft only if you have room to spare after installing more important devices.

Balloon Stills. Tricky and needing constant attention, but they work. Stills represent the lowest possible technology. They can be repaired if damaged and, if you have enough of them, will keep you and your crew alive. They are a bit hard to find, as the military discontinued them. If you find a cache, buy all you can get.

Rain Catchment. Most long survival episodes occur in the tradewind belts, where there can be long periods with little serious rain. Catchment devices designed by the raftmakers rarely work, and fail to consider that the catchment itself will be fouled by salt. On one epic survival passage, the sun and the sea decomposed the catchment device, and fouled the pure rainwater that fell into it. Devise your own rain catchment device out of a space blanket. Mylar will not disintegrate and you have the additional advantage of its use for warmth at night.

Reverse Osmosis. The new, hand-powered, reverse-osmosis devices will deliver sufficient pure water to keep you alive. One of these examples of engineering legerdemain should be carried on every offshore raft. It is the almost perfect, if expensive, solution.

There are two disadvantages. The first is that physical energy is required, of which there might be little left after abandoning ship. But if you need the water you will find the strength to operate it. The other disadvantage is that they are high-tech devices and are essentially unrepairable. The filtering membrane is extremely delicate and any fouling, by suspended iron particles or by oil in the sea, will diminish its efficiency and deliver brackish water or cause it to fail altogether. While reverse-osmosis devices should be carried, they must be regarded as a water source of last resort.

Squeeze a Fish. There are potable supplies of fresh water in the bodies of all fish. The liquids squeezed out of a fish, while salty, are sweet enough to provide needed liquid. A small garlic press will do the trick. The best source is the aqueous humor contained inside the fish eyes. Not for the squeamish, but the experience of those who have been there teaches that squeamishness disappears early.

Of all available systems, the balloon still, with all of its problems, remains the water-source of last resort. After you have drunk all of the cans, fouled your osmosis filter, are rainless and fishless, these little rubber balloons will sustain life.

Liferaft Repair

Try this little experiment. Take an inflated inner tube and a repair kit like the one found in your liferaft into a swimming pool. Punch a hole in the tube and attempt an airtight repair while in the water. You will be wet, your repair kit will be wet, and the tube will be wet and flabby and difficult to hold. Then, instead of a small hole, cut a ragged six-inch slash into the tube, as might occur in an encounter with a sharp object or a determined shark. Now try to effect a repair. If you have been successful in the pool (I never have), remember that in real life you would be in rough seas, tired, scared, cold, and weak from exertion and inadequate sustenance. The purpose of this scenario is to emphasize the criminal inadequacy of the repair and maintenance facilities with which you are supposed to keep your frail craft afloat. With what you are given, a liferaft is almost impossible to repair.

MECHANICAL REPAIR TECHNIQUES

In the two examples illustrated here, A and B, both can be accomplished under difficult circumstances. It is not easy, but it is possible, and the repair is relatively permanent.

Small Hole Repair. For punctures and small holes, a device as in illustration A should be constructed. The backing plate is oval so that it may be slipped into a round hole and still retain the capacity to seal. A small dab of silicone sealant would help, but the device will work adequately with only its own mechanical seal.

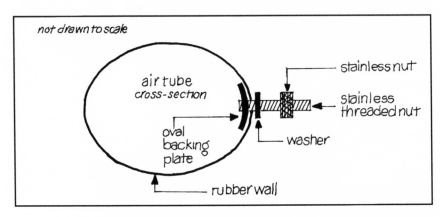

A. Using a backing plug and tightening device.

Large Opening Repair. For larger holes, slashes, or irregular punctures, the method illustrated in B is most effective. The tube is first deflated and the material around the damaged area is then gathered around a wooden dowel. This is tightly whipped, using whipping twine or heavy nylon fishing line. A small supply of dowels of different diameters should be carried along with plenty of whipping twine.

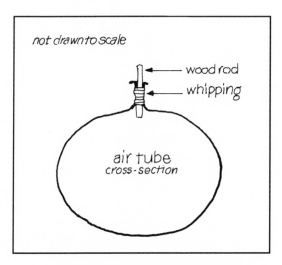

B. A whipped repair using a rod core.

With only a bit of small line, and almost anything that can be used as a core, this repair technique is available to the most ill-equipped raft. Should damage to a tube be really extensive, the entire tube can be sealed at both ends like a sausage.

A bit of rubber, trimmed from the edge of the damaged area, and wrapped under the whipping closest to the tube wall, will prevent chafing and will act as a "waste" that can be replaced as needed.

Food Supply

Most rafts are supplied with a fishing line and hooks, although experience has taught that it is well nigh impossible to inveigle a fish at sea to take a hook from a raft. Deep ocean fish are accustomed to eating their dinners live, and they look with disdain and suspicion at a hook dangling under a raft baited with a chunk of who knows what.

THE BEST WAY TO CATCH A FISH

On a raft the only way to consistently take fish is by spearing them. The best device is a small, stainless steel, barbed trident and a folding stainless gaff. You will need a folding or detachable handle for the trident to extend your reach, and a line with which to rescue the trident when the speared fish pulls it out of your hands. You will also need a heavy object with which to subdue the fish before you bring it aboard lest, in its thrashings, it puts the pointy ends of your trident through an air tube. If you have alcohol aboard, a dollop in the gills will instantly quiet the most exuberant fish. Never try to take a fish that is bigger than a bread box. It will do more damage to you and your little home than it is worth.

SHOOTING FISH IN A BARREL

A 38-caliber shell discharged into the water near a fish will stun it and, if you are lucky it will float to the surface. I would not recommend carrying a revolver on a raft for the sole purpose of taking fish, but since there are a number of emergency and signaling uses for a gun, it is an option worth keeping in mind.

38-CALIBER BIRDSHOT

Shells for your 38 revolver can be had with a capsule of birdshot replacing the lead slug. This will easily bring down a bird at a reasonable range. There also exists a barrel insert for your 25-mm flare gun that will take a 410 shotgun shell with a birdshot load. This insert will take birds at relatively long range.

PLANKTON

You can live as well as whales do on plankton alone. You will need a plankton net, a number of spares, and some repair material. The nets are 5" in diameter and have a stainless steel hoop. The net size should be between 300 and 500 microns. Remember that plankton rise to the surface mostly at night, and in some oceans are not always present in quantities sufficient to maintain life.

Food supplies that you have stashed away on your raft will most likely be your primary diet till rescued. Be wary of packing emergency foods with high-protein content. The higher a protein diet, the more water you will need. A freshly caught fish supplies some of the liquid that your body will need to absorb its protein. You must have the proper tools with which to harvest it.

Signaling

Those who have been cast away at sea consistently report that ship after ship passed them by. The attention of those on the warm, closed bridge of a big ship far at sea must be attracted by the use of much more heroic methods than those we generally have available to us on a raft. With the ubiquitousness of aircraft and satellites it is possible that rescues will be faster and more frequent in the future, but for these we need special equipment. Here are the signaling options ranging from the highest to the lowest tech devices.

EPIRB

No emergency package should be without an EPIRB (Emergency Position Indicating Radio Beacon), although it is high-tech, which I mistrust on a raft. It is your best chance of being found quickly and, in fact, it is the basis of the military's "find 'em fast or forget 'em" attitude. An EPIRB is not restricted to use aboard a liferaft, although it comes in a nice waterproof package designed for just that use. If you feel that you are not in a survivable condition, you can resort to the EPIRB while still aboard your boat. (Ask any radio technician how you can enhance the emergency battery built into the EPIRB by using your boat's 12-volt batteries while still aboard, and thus preserve the EPIRB's power supply in the event that you have to take to your liferaft.) If you are in a reasonably well-traveled air corridor, do not wait until a plane is sighted before activating your EPIRB. Most flights that are within radio range will be out of sight, so turn it on and *leave it on*.

HAND-HELD VHF RADIO

There are relatively inexpensive, hand-held radios that operate on Emergency Channel 16. All ships at sea are supposed to be tuned to that channel. Alas, frequently they are not. These radios, if stored unused for a long time in your raft container, are not dependable. If you plan to include a Channel 16 radio as liferaft gear, take one that has been in daily use aboard your boat. Should you sight a ship, start immediately with the call, "Mayday, Mayday," and repeat until they acknowledge you. If they are minding the channel, acknowledgment will be quick. If not, save your batteries and try another signaling method. When they work, and when the big ships are listening, these radios are wonderful.

DYE MARKER POWDER

Light, cheap, and highly visible to overflying planes. Extremely useful after an aircraft has detected your EPIRB signal and is searching for you.

SIGNALING MIRROR

An effective, easily carried, and easily used device. On a bright, sunny day, if the passing ship is between you and the sun, a very strong light can be directed its way. Get one and practice a bit.

FLARES

Flares recommended to yachtsmen are overrated as a signaling device and, to add insult to injury, they often do not work. When they do work they are rarely noticed. You cannot depend on the pipsqueak, 25-mm sparklers that are sold to yachtsmen. In any kind of big sea, which is usually accompanied by limited visibility, they are too weak and too short-lived to attract much attention. Use only military issue 50-mm parachute flares. They go way up, are very bright, and stay up for a long time.

GUNS

Especially at night, if your flares have gone unnoticed, and a big boat is passing you at close range, put six rounds into the side of the iron monster. Gunshots can be heard across a very long distance at sea and the clang of lead on steel should attract someone's attention. Besides, you will feel better for having shot at them in the event they fail to stop.

These are the basic requirements and changes that should be incorporated into any offshore liferaft. If you have a large crew, more than four, you might consider carrying two six-person rafts, but this is expensive. Almost all boats today carry some kind of inflatable dinghy. Remember to consider this as a backup emergency raft.

EMERGENCIES

The First Ten Seconds

Three bad things can happen to you on a small boat anywhere in the world at any time. A crewmember can fall overboard, a fire can occur, or you can bump into something hard. No delay must be allowed in dealing with these eventualities.

As terrible as they sound, only a tiny percentage of yachtsmen are ever lost to these three bad things, far fewer than are lost in airline accidents—even if the comparison is made in minutes of travel time. Life-threatening events can be substantially reduced by preparation. And preparation means drill.

But immediately preceding the drills themselves, there is a tiny and crucial patch of time that is the stuff of life itself. Disaster is either assured or avoided during the first ten seconds of an emergency. If those precious seconds are used to put into effect carefully rehearsed drills, it would take a bucket of bad luck to get anybody killed. The problem aboard most boats in bad trouble is that these irreplaceable first seconds are expended in flailing about. As the emergency unfolds, there will be time enough to sort things out rationally and calmly, but only if the first ten seconds have been put to good use.

The purpose of the first ten seconds is to set the stage for the drill to happen. The first ten seconds are the only real, quality time of the drill. All the rest is commentary, rote, and training.

THE GREATER TEN-SECOND EMERGENCIES

Fire. In the first ten seconds after a fire is discovered the immediate and proper response is:

The skipper activates the extinguisher *nearest to the flames.*

A crewmember approaches from the end of the boat opposite from the skipper and activates the extinguisher *nearest
to the flames* from that side.

A crewmember throws all containers of gasoline overboard
and attaches lines or floats to propane tanks and sets them
adrift.

A crewmember stands by the liferaft and prepares to move
it should the fire spread.

In the first ten seconds you have now done everything possible
to assure that you will survive the fire. The natural inclination,
at the cry of "fire," is to grab the extinguisher nearest you. This
is wrong. The extinguishers nearest to the flames are used first
so that you will not lose them should the fire spread. Gasoline
and propane are deep-sixed because boats that would easily survive a bad fire would not survive an explosion. Evacuating your
liferaft from the path of the flames is your assurance that,
should the fire get out of control, you will not watch it eat up
your best remaining chance of survival.

Man Overboard. Upon witnessing or discovering a crew in the
water, the first necessary act is that the helmsman *note and write
down compass course, speed, and time.* With this information
the boat can be brought about to return to the spot where absence was first noted. The spot at which discovery of absence is
made is always the spot closest to the overboard crew, no matter if he went over a minute or an hour before. That is the spot
that must be absolutely and immediately noted by the helmsman. It is your only and best point of reference.

THE LESSER TEN-SECOND EMERGENCIES

There are two other events that call for immediate, ten-second action, but are not as serious a threat to the survival of the vessel.

Broken Stay or Shroud. Should a stay or shroud go, the instant first ten-second response must be to turn the boat so that the broken cable is to lee, thus allowing wind pressure to reinforce the mast rather than adding to the threat.

Burns. Should a crew suffer a serious burn, the first ten-second response is to fully douse the burn with cold water to prevent further "cooking," and then to immediately get codeine into the patient to prevent shock.

Too Specific Emergency Advice

There are googols of goodies written about what to do should the moon fall on your head or should St. Elmo's Fire get into your firecracker stash. Most of the directions concerning emergencies at sea are quite good. Most, unfortunately, go into too much detail for a sailor, caught in an emergency, to remember.

OFFSHORE VERSUS LONGSHORE EMERGENCIES

The open sea provides the luxury of time in dealing with emergencies. At sea, we are able to narrowly concentrate our energies on the actual emergency, with little concern for shallow waters, dangers to navigation, or threatening traffic. The first-time, offshore passagemaker can take comfort from the fact that it is demonstrably safer to deal with an emergency situation a thousand miles at sea than it is a thousand feet off a breaking surf. The land is ever the sailor's enemy, and never more so than when there is trouble.

HOW TO THINK ABOUT EMERGENCIES

In thinking about emergencies, we must first realize how they numb and paralyze us. Time slows down and we helplessly observe the developing debacle, unable to remember damn-all what to do about it. If lucky we respond unthinkingly and, if doubly lucky, our response is the correct one out of the many we could have made. More times than not, during the irretrievable first few seconds, we passively watch events unfold as we are thrown to the lions of chance. Human beings are really lousy in emergencies. Quick, overwhelming, and unexpected attacks are usually met with slack-jawed paralysis. We are, however, swell at thinking about problems. Give us a little time and we will un-kink any knot, but to be able to act instantly, we must develop mindless and automatic rejoinders to trouble. These must be few enough that we will remember them, and they must relieve the emergency just enough to get us through the initial be-numbment, and across the bar to quieter waters wherein we can think more rationally about our problem.

CATEGORIES OF DISASTERS

In order to start on this admittedly large order, we must remind ourselves that threats vary according to their immediacy. There are some that need instant, screaming, total response. The rest are emergencies for which we might be able to use a band-aid until we have some time to consider less-pressured solutions. We must also recognize that emergencies have internally ranked hierarchies of hazard. Calamitous events that need some kind of instant response do not always require an instantaneous, com-plete solution for the whole emergency. Usually what is required to counter a life-threatening series of events (they never come singly) is that you go below, put your feet up, and think about it. The forestalling of more damage we have described as the first ten-second response.

Thinking about emergencies *before* they happen is the best way to deal with them. Anything that you can accomplish to make a possible emergency more amenable to resolution re-quires that much less time and panicky effort in the event. For example, in case of a fire, where you place extinguishers is as important as having them in the first place.

THE INDIVISIBLE OFFSHORE EMERGENCY: FIRE

Fire is a total, progressive, and indivisible offshore emergency. There is no possibility of timely assistance from others and, unchecked, any fire can cost you your life as well as your ship. The only response to a fire is to put it out at all costs. The only means you have to put it out are your fire extinguishers. *Finding your fire extinguishers is as important as having them.* Drill everyone so that at the first hint of fire they will go immediately to the extinguishers and only then to the fire. Then drill them again.

Three things that you can do in advance:

> *Use only Halon* type extinguishers. They almost never leak, are always ready, and do not make a mess. Delay due to the reluctance to make a mess has burned many boats to their waterline.

> *Place extinguishers* on *both* sides of every doorway so that no matter from which direction you might approach a fire, you will have an extinguisher that is not already red hot.

> *You are going offshore* and you might be at sea for a month. You may have more than one fire, so buy many more extinguishers than you think you will need, and more than you can afford.

DIVISIBLE EMERGENCIES

Man Overboard. When a crew goes overboard the chances are that you will not actually see him go into the water. If you should see the event, in any kind of sea you will lose sight of him within ten seconds. With the choice between watching the crew in the water, or establishing your position, do not waste precious seconds maintaining sight of him in the water. The proper response is to *immediately establish your position, course, and time*. If you are not sure when the incident occurred, and in many cases the people remaining aboard are not, then the only thing that you can know positively is where the boat is at the moment that you become aware of the problem. That will be your starting point for the search, and if you do not immediately establish your own position, it will become difficult, if not impossible, to retrace the piece of ocean in which your crew might still be floating.

The first ten-seconds' reaction of establishing position will give you a breather to start the search in a deliberate and calm manner. After establishing your position and time, you must start the familiar and well-documented procedure for: 1) promptly and safely reversing course, 2) determining the changed influence of leeway, and 3) commencing the actual search itself. How far back over your course you go is hard to advise. It depends on your best estimate of when the crew went into the water. If he was alone on watch then you must retrace his last DR entry which, if he was attending to duty, should be no more than six or seven miles back (one hour in the log book). Details of careful search patterns and procedures can be found in many books on safety at sea. Adopt one method as your own and apply it in drills.

Note that continuously throwing stuff overboard that has little windage (like some cushions) and will not be blown to lee (like pages torn out of a magazine) can be enormously helpful in defining, both for you and for the man in the water, where you have been and where you are likely to meet.

The temptation is to peer intently over your bows for the missing man. Abandon your bows and station your crew looking to port and starboard. You will more likely pass your man overboard to one side or the other than you will come upon him from dead ahead.

Broken Headstay. Should your headstay part, put the wind be-hind you without a jibe. This should hold the mast in place until you can effect repairs. Then slow the boat to reduce rolling and pitching, and use jib halyards and spinnaker halyards to stay the mast forward. Do not take down or reef the main until hal-yards are firmly in place, lest the increased motion resulting from lowered sails further destabilizes the mast.

Broken Backstay. Come into the wind very slowly. The purpose of this maneuver is to create wind support for the mast. The best point of sail is close off the wind. Directly into the wind there will be too much undamped motion. Then run your jib halyards aft around the mast to the stern. Use two halyards and attach them astern as far port and starboard as possible. Do not use the topping lift. You will need the topping lift to maintain the trim of the mainsail, which is creating the aftward support for the mast. Do not reef or lower the main for fear of increas-ing undamped motion until the mast is stayed.

Broken Shrouds. Put the wind opposite the parted stay. Avoid a jibe. In very calm seas you may put your boom out the side op-posite the parted stay to act as a low-level spreader using a jib halyard as a shroud. Since shrouds are more likely to part in rough rather than in calm waters you must maintain the sup-porting pressure of the mainsail on the mast while avoiding the strains caused by dipping a winged-out boom into the water. If you are lucky and the shroud has parted near the deck, make an eye with cable clamps and reattach the shroud with a block and tackle, or tension with a winch. Free the winch as soon as pos-sible as you will be needing it to control the trim of your sails.

Dismasting. Prevent further damage. If the mast is overboard re-trieve it before it holes you. If it is on deck secure it. If this is not possible cut it free. If the mast is free in the water and you are unable to bring it immediately on deck, sink it on a long, very

Surviving a dismasting in the Red Sea.

strong line. It may provide some benefit as a sea anchor, and you can retrieve it later for use in a jury rig.

Line Around the Propeller. Stop all forward motion in preparation for putting someone in the water. Do not restart engine. Do not *ever* attempt to free the prop by going into reverse. Tie your crew firmly to the boat, put out your boarding ladder, and send him slowly into the water with a sharp knife and a hacksaw. A fouled line can almost never be untangled. Do not try. Cut it. When the prop is free *and crew is back on board*, restart the engine and very slowly engage the gear and increase the RPMs. Listen for vibrations from a bent shaft often associated with a fouled propeller.

It all started with blue-eyed Ellie.

Blue-eyed Ellie was born in Poland in the wrong year and to the wrong parents. He lived out the war, in terror and in hiding, in occupied France. He ultimately became respected and successful in the academic world but he never lost his talent for caution or his instinct for survival and self protection.

Blue-eyed Ellie finally emigrated from his beloved France to Israel for reasons not even altogether clear to himself. I found him there hammering away at an old iron boat. I came to love Ellie, as did everyone. He had retired from the University and was, at 60, preparing for ocean passages. When, half in jest, I asked him to sail with me down the Red Sea and on toward Australia, his caution and conservatism abandoned him and, to my surprise, to his surprise and to the collective surprise of all who knew of his passion for remaining out of harm's way, he instantly agreed.

Blue-eyed Ellie stood by his commitment although he soon was overwhelmed with the need to make the passage as safe as possible. He appointed himself navigator and planned precise passages to minutes on the clock and yards in the sea. He appointed himself rigger and, though over 60, he clambered and climbed about the rigging, supple as a bamboo shoot, in a frenzy of inspection. He had become plucky, but not foolish. He was covering his cautious French derrière.

But this yarn is not about blue-eyed Ellie, though it well could be. It is about David, his friend, and it is about the most inappropriate task ever laid on me.

In his passion for anticipating any possible upcoming confront, blue-eyed Ellie asked to see my arms chest. He was unimpressed with my ancient shotgun. What I needed, this small and civilized and gentle Frenchman declared, was a serious weapon . . . something fully automatic with which I could protect us in the Red Sea when the Arab fanatics would come for his carefully preserved Israeli hide. I was appointed gunsel for Ellie.

Automatic weapons cannot be bought in Israel but blue-eyed Ellie had a friend who had a Kalashnikov rifle, an AK47, the best and most terrible automatic weapon ever built. He was intent that his friend loan it to us. But the friend, David, had a problem. David, having fought effectively in every Israeli war since 1947, had evolved into a passionate pacifist. He could no longer live with the thought that any gun of his might be used in a warlike manner. And how else can one use a Kalashnikov?

On the other hand, in the best Talmudic tradition, David agonized over his responsibility to us lest we sail off without the Kalashnikov and be set upon by savage hordes. Ultimately he gave in to his need to see us "protected." He presented me with the Kalashnikov and, at the same time, made a nice little rabbinic suggestion which got him neatly off the pointy horns of his dilemma.

"I give you this weapon of war which is intended to kill and maim my fellow man," David formally declared. "I give it to you upon the condition that, although it is a weapon of war, you must find a peaceful use for it."

Now I ask you, how do you find a peaceful use for a gun that never jams, will empty a fifty-round clip in seconds and was designed, specifically, to cut a man in half? I accepted the weapon for nervous Ellie's sake and with crossed fingers accepted David's charge that I discover a peaceful use. Ha!

We sailed off from Israel, headed down through the Suez and in the Red Sea, between Yemen and Ethiopia. A harder rock and a harder place would be impossible to find. Our mast broke off at twenty feet above deck. It hung by its internal wires and cables and halyards from the remaining stub, banging merrily against our hull to the tune of an unpleasant sea. The hanging mast section had to come down lest it do us further damage. There was, however, no way to send anyone aloft to cut it down lest the cut away mast and flailing cables remove some part of the person doing the cutting. A dilemma indeed.

I pondered the matter and hit upon a scheme that solved both my immediate, dangerous dilemma and David's moral one. I went below, shoved a full clip into David's Kalashnikov, came on deck, braced myself, switched the gun to full automatic and blazed away at the offending cables. It only took a second and the mast slid quietly into the sea. The Kalashnikov, like a giant pair of scissors, had sheared them away.

My mast was in the sea. My dilemma was solved. And, against all odds, I had obeyed David's injunction to find a 'peaceful use' for his murderous gun.

In the Red Sea, as ancient history teaches, anything can happen.

THE UNLIKELIHOOD OF ILLNESS

Our society encases us in a swaddle of health-care facilities. The inventory of immediately available medical assistance would encourage a visitor from Mars to believe that we are all on the brink of physical dissolution and that we are only kept from the final pit by an endless array of medical props.

The fact is that living things in general, and humans in particular, are remarkably resistant machines. So long as we accept the dictatorial hegemony of our genes that lie in ambush awaiting us, we go on from day to month to decade with relatively little need for repair.

Medical props loom over us as we are just about toes-up. The startling statistic is that about half of U.S. medical dollars are spent in the last year of life. Half of all our medical billions buys each of us only one more year.

So unless you are over 75, deep in heart failure, *and* on a dialysis machine, the chances are very good that a couple of weeks out of the sight of land will not represent an irrational health risk. Certainly you will be less in harm's way, both physically and medically, by not being immersed in the miasmas and the violences of land, where breathing the air, drinking the water, driving to work, or becoming a crime statistic define modern urban life.

It is not the fear of sickness at sea that keeps us landbound, it is our terror at being separated from the instant medicine to which we have become unnecessarily accustomed. Too many hospital beds, too many physicians and specialists, too many clinics, emergency rooms, drugstores, and too damn much daily and ever-changing media fads have built the fiction in our minds that we are an unhealthy lot in constant need of medical care.

A heart attack will as likely kill you on land as it will at sea. Granted, the length of time away from intensive care increases the likelihood that an attack will be fatal. But most heart patients have lots of warning and if you are a victim you should weigh the plusses and the minuses before going to sea for a long period.

Aside from a massive coronary there is little else in the dreary litany of illness that will favor killing you at sea over killing you on land.

Except for trauma, which happens less on a sailboat than on land, most illnesses creep up on you and you can wait them out, perhaps uncomfortably, until you reach port.

It is the shock that accompanies trauma that is the killer. The shock emerges from the pain of the wounding so that you must control pain. Carry lots of heavy duty pain killers and use them heavily before the pain becomes the killer. Codeine is great but ask your doctor.

So you never know.

The moment of truth came when we were on the short but sometimes troublesome passage from Cuba to Key West. Mar and I had invited a pair of ladies to sail with us. They had just bought a catamaran and wanted some ocean experience. They had a couple of years of coastwise catamaran sailing but were timid about, as they said, "going overseas."

As catamaran sailors they were not exactly anticipating the special motion of a monohull and, as long as they were carefully seated in the cockpit, all was well.

At a certain moment nature called and one of the ladies went below just as we began to feel the press of the Gulf Stream. She walked about freely below, as if on a catamaran, and, as a result, was tossed violently about, sustained a hit on the head, and landed on a bunk.

Good thing too, since the woman who lay unconscious weighed something over two of me and there was no way that she could have been picked off the deck by Mar who was a third of her weight. I was on the wheel, the seas were becoming boisterous, the big woman's friend was terrified and Mar was below with a now reviving but very confused and concussed woman.

I watched with amazement as Mar started the exact medical regimen for dealing with a concussion. She was very severe, would not let the patient lie down, and kept her wide awake for the eight hours that it took to get us back to Havana.

When the Cuban medical team picked up the patient they told me that Mar had prevented further damage and probably saved the woman's life. Where, they asked, did she learn her medical skills? Was she a nurse or a doctor? How did she know exactly what to do?

I was even more puzzled than they because I knew that Mar had never even had a first-aid course. Here was a mystery and a new and surprising facet to my wife that I had never even suspected.

Later I asked what other medical skills she was hiding from me.

"What in the world do you mean?" she replied.

"You obviously knew exactly what to do to save that poor woman," I answered, getting a bit peeved at having missed all knowledge of this special medical training, "where, and more to the point, when did you get medically trained to know how to handle a concussion?"

Mar looked puzzled for a moment and then burst out into a peal of pure laughter.

"You will never believe it," she said.

"Try me," I urged.

"Well, you are going to laugh at me."

"No, no, I am really impressed. Now how much training have you had?"

"Remember M*A*S*H*? " she asked.

"Sure, a favorite of mine."

Then with a puckish giggle she said, "Remember the episode when Hawkeye turned his Jeep over and had to spend a whole night in a Korean hut keeping himself awake because he had a concussion?"

A light bulb flashed on over my head, "You mean . . ." I sputtered.

"Yep, I just did what Hawkeye did."

You never know when a stray bit of wisdom picked up *en passant* can save a life.

A special case of trauma is burn. Extremely painful, so treat burns early with pain medication, since shock, induced by pain, is more likely to kill you than is the burn trauma itself. Additionally burns are subject to infection and are difficult to bandage. To prevent infection my absolute requirement for burn is a cream composed of sulfa drugs and metallic silver. It is called Silvadene. Carry it. Carry lots.

We were setting off from the States toward our first leg of a proposed circumnavigation. This first leg was a doozer, 4000 empty miles between Panama and Tahiti. We had to be entirely self sufficient for possibly three months.

Before setting off I turned to Gilbert, "my son the Doctor," for medical supplies. He proposed everything short of an iron lung; all of the goodies were stored aboard awaiting endless medical calamities. Most of the drugs were never called upon to perform and that gave me my first hint that sailors at sea rarely have arcane diseases creep up upon them.

However, calamity did indeed strike. It was in the form of a serious burn that I sustained halfway between Panama and the Society Isles which, at that point, were still three weeks away.

One lovely dawn I had been dallying with my lady (or she with me) on deck in the comforting folds of a tied down jenny. I was without clothing, a normal condition aboard even absent dalliance, as I went below to prepare breakfast.

Still nude, in spite of an oilcloth apron hanging handily at the stove, I started the alcohol stove which, as was its habit now and then, caught and then died leaving a hot burner. Rather than taking the time to allow it to cool, I squirted more alcohol from a squeeze bottle onto the burner. Physics and chemistry being what they are, the stream of alcohol hit and was ignited by the hot burner and flamed back up to the squeeze bottle. I tried to toss the bottle away from my bare body but the bottle turned lazily in the air spraying burning alcohol from just below my jewels to my insteps.

My lady, reacting faster than I could, grabbed a readied bottle of cold water and doused the flames along both my legs, thus cooling and halting more damage.

(Much later, after things settled down, she said that, as I came up from the galley with blue flames along both legs, I "looked like a shish kebab.") There I was, weeks from medical asistance with substantial second degree burns. My survival now depended on the Universe.

The first thing we did right was to lace me with codeine to prevent shock.

The second thing we did right was to turn on our world-circling amateur radio and call for someone to hook me up with my son in far away Philadelphia. My medical emergency call was picked up by an amateur in Texas and the emergency frequency he found me on was kept free all around the world for the balance of the time of my emergency.

With codeine induced ability I croaked, "Call Gil Palley by phone in Philadelphia," and I gave his number.

"No problem," the welcome Texas drawl came back and within ten minutes after my accident the Texas amateur had patched me into the U.S. phone system and I was talking directly to my son.

Gil called immediately the burn center at the University of Pennsylvania hospital. The trauma physician on duty asked if I had Silvadene aboard.

Now let us look back to some weeks earlier when Gil was medically stocking my boat. He had brought a large jar of Silvadene aboard with the rest of the medicaments and came back the next day with four more large jars. When I asked why so much he shrugged and said, "I dont know why but I just had this powerful feeling that more might be needed." The one big jar was enough Silvadene for a half body burn. Four more just seemed too much but I stored them away anyway.

Back to mid-Pacific. The burn center asked how long before I could get to a hospital. I said three weeks and there was a depressing silence. When I told them that I had five huge jars of Silvadene aboard the clouds lifted. I was told by them that one jar would last about four days.

Three weeks later, on my last jar of Silvadene, we made harbor at Hiva Oa in the Marquesas. A physician on the island, who inspected my burns, declared me cured.

The Universe works in mysterious ways. Most of the time I get the sure notion that the Universe is conspiring against me and it often is in what turns out to be mostly minor matters. But when the chips are down and toes are on the way up, sometimes, just sometimes, the Universe relents with such clarity that it is hard to believe that its actions are entirely accidental. Even Einstein refused to believe that the Universe was "shooting craps" with us.

Preventative medicine

The medical world finally discovered that keeping us healthy is a more rational, humane, and cheaper method of practicing medicine than curing us after we get sick. The same principle can operate on a long passage. The skipper's preventative functions are:

> Prior to departure the skipper obtains medical histories of all crew detailing past events which might throw light on future medical or emotional problems.
>
> The skipper obtains a complete record of blood types and is aware of any existing allergies to either medications or foodstuffs.
>
> The skipper functions as a nutritionist and makes sure that a proper and healthy diet is both supplied and eaten.
>
> The skipper, as the sole dispenser of drugs and medicines, holds a daily "sick call." Medical problems are not left to be dealt with individually by the crew. On sick call the skipper is alert for those small medical matters which might later loom large and over which a crewmember might be reluctant to make a fuss. Small discomforts, if relieved early, make for a more pleasant passage, and larger problems, which could become serious, can possibly be kept under medical control until land is reached. The sick call becomes a part of a daily immutable routine and includes the entire crew, whether or not any have complaints.

On land a temporary sick day is no big deal since there are always more folk around to do a job than are really necessary. But aboard ship, where the whole universe might consist only of four people, all absences are keenly felt and the holes never quite close. So it behooves the skipper to keep all aboard well and functional. Each member of the small crew on a small sailing vessel is very important indeed.

CHAPTER **6**

Navigation

THE COMPASS

To most of us, a compass is truth and direction revealed. It is like that bright star that guided the shepherds, without error, across the sands of Judea to Bethlehem. We set our sights by our compass. We take our course from our compass. Every boy scout knows that when you get lost in the woods all you need is a compass for salvation.

But as it is with most common knowledge, the popular view of the compass is wrong. The compass is *never* right. It is always wrong to some larger or lesser degree. A compass has never led anyone without error to his goal. A compass is like the charismatic leader whom the public blindly follows. Both leader and compass are more image than substance.

It is no less a miracle that the Wise Men arrived in Bethlehem than it is that any compass ever led anybody anywhere. The compass works only as the result of the investment of an astounding amount of past human labor and continues to work only because committed people still check, recheck, correct, and worry about this magic, perverse, little bubble.

True or Geographic North versus Magnetic North

Every square foot of the earth's surface has a slightly different orientation to geographic north than a compass, pointing to magnetic north, will indicate. Not only does the compass almost never point north, but the amount it varies from north at any place on earth constantly changes.

A magnetic compass is a mute slave to the least touchable, most quivery natural force that we have so far discovered. We neither know how magnetism works nor how to significantly alter or control it. What we do know is that, if we put oil in a saucer and carefully float an iron needle in it, the needle will always point in a unique direction and, if the saucer is rotated, will continue to return to that direction if given enough time. If we should wait too long, say a decade or two, it is likely that the needle will find a new direction to point to, as magnetic north floats around in the Arctic.

Magnetic Anomalies and Other Errors

We also have to be careful where on earth we place the little needle. In addition to the normal inclination of magnetic north to wander, there are places on earth that have been identified as having different magnetic influences than we might expect. In addition to the needle wandering about in response to the slow shifts of the earth's magnetic north, it also reacts to smaller stuff closer at hand: a lode of iron ore (creating a magnetic anomaly) as big as the Ritz buried half a mile beneath you, a flashlight, or your old non-stainless steel bos'n's knife lying half a foot away.

It is only because we are so incredibly stubborn that, once having decided the compass was truth, we were damn well going to make it work. The only reason why the whole pulsing and shifting and wriggling phenomenon that we call magnetic direction finding works at all is because our compulsive ances-

tors spent the last half millennia identifying and removing magnetic errors from every spot on earth. And we must keep cor-
recting because even those slippery errors, once identified, keep
sliding about every few years.

VARIATION

One group of errors to which the compass is subject is due to
the fact that the Lord was too busy making earth and water and
us to arrange that the magnetic north be located where it belongs—right at the north pole instead of some hundreds of
miles from the familiar geographic north of your globe.

This manner in which a compass varies from true north is
called, with uncharacteristic logic, variation. Variation has been
carefully plotted so that you can know how many degrees to add
to or subtract from your compass reading depending on where
on the earth you happen to be. Pilot charts have little gray lines
that represent "lines of equal variation." Along these lines the
variation error of your compass is the same. If you should happen to be sailing near a line that says, for example, 13°, then you
will have to either add or subtract that figure to the reading
your compass is displaying in order to determine where in the
world true north is. Thirteen degrees of error may sound like a
lot for an instrument that, when you woke up this morning, you
were convinced was accurate and dependable. Thirteen degrees
is *nothing*. There are places where the error rises to a stark fifty
degrees and changes faster than latitude and longitude! Try navigating with that.

VARIATION ANNUAL CHANGE

In most of the waters you will sail, variation error will rarely
rise above 15°. But, as I hinted before, even these values are not
fixed. To determine the annual change in variation at any point
on the globe you happen to be, you must determine (1) what

was the last year that the variation was measured, (2) how much each year it will increase or decrease and, (3) whether it will change toward east or toward west. For this information you must go to any larger scale chart, more local and detailed, and with a magnetic compass rose printed on it.

Deviation

We must now deal with the fact that the compass mounted on your boat has a different error included with each different degree, depending on the amount of iron you have strewn around it. Your engine, the water tank in your port cockpit locker—not to mention the stern anchor lashed to the pushpit *and* the pushpit itself—all beckon, Circe-like, your compass to incline toward them. This introduces an additional error called deviation, which is in your power to alter.

ADJUSTING AND COMPENSATING FOR DEVIATION ERROR

After you get all your ferrous foolishness stowed as far away from your compass as possible, it will be necessary to bring a compass adjuster aboard who will use the sun and the stars to find out how much onboard error (deviation) your boat has. The adjuster will reduce this error, not the same for all points of the compass, as much as possible by playing a sort of musical chairs with the little compensation magnets cunningly hidden beneath the compass housing. Then, along with a large bill, you will receive a compass deviation card that tells you how much error, east or west, is present for each of the 16 points of your compass. If the deviation error is never more than about three degrees or so, throw the card away and declare your compass deviationally perfect. But if the uncorrected error in any direction is substantial, you must grind these uncompensated deviation errors into your course calculations.

From here on and till the end of time, boy scout knives, pocket radios, flashlights, and anything else of steel, are banned from cuddling with the compass. Excepting only stainless steel which, if it is of sufficiently high quality, has been purged of its ability to pulse your pointer.

DETECTING UNCOMPENSATED DEVIATION ERROR AT SEA

For the purpose of our offshore passage we will assume that the compass has been adjusted before departure. But in the course of a long passage and all of the knocking about implied, it is possible that your onboard error, your deviation error, has changed. To determine this mid-ocean, *sans* geographical references or knowledge of rising and setting azimuths, requires only the simplest of tests.

Observe your compass. In its center there is a vertical pin that, if the sun is low enough in the sky, will cast a shadow out to the numerical markings on the edge of the card. Point your boat to 360° and write down the bearing upon which the pin's shadow falls. Within a ten-minute period (less is better) do the same for each 45° around the compass card. You will end up with eight numbers. If no two of these numbers are more than 10° apart, it means that the maximum deviation error in your compass does not anywhere exceed 5°. This assures you that no large and potentially disastrous deviation has crept in. Since you do not steer with much more overall accuracy than 5°, you can live with this much error. If the deviation should exceed 5°, search out the iron imp that is responsible and ban the ferrous fellow from the binnacle.

CHANGING COMPASS TO TRUE AND TRUE TO COMPASS

So far we have learned that a compass placed anywhere on earth has both variation error, due to the many miles between true polar north and magnetic north, and deviation error, due to ferrous material present on your boat. Both of these errors must be accounted for in changing a magnetic compass heading to a geographically true heading, or the converse. In order to do this mindlessly, memorize this embarrassing little piece of doggerel:

Can Dead Men Vote Twice—add East

This instructs us that, when converting a magnetic compass reading to a geographic true direction on a chart, you must add deviation error and variation error so long as they are both east errors. Should they both be west errors you will subtract both. Should one be an east error and one a west error, you will add east and subtract west. If you want to go in the other direction and determine what compass reading will be equivalent to a true notation on a chart, then simply reverse everything. In this case you subtract east and add west, etc. Do not ask why. Just do it. It works every time.

(The (M) stands for the magnetic heading, which is no more than what your compass (C) reads corrected for either deviation (D) or variation (V) depending on whether you are going from compass (C) to true (T) or from true (T) to compass (C). Never both. Do not memorize anything but the doggerel. All of the additions and subtractions of east and west errors can be logically deduced from that.)

When Compasses Work Best

With all of this error and confusion and endless change, how come we still have an unshakable belief in our compasses? Why has nothing yet replaced this ubiquitous, if erroneous, little bubblehead? The answer is that, in spite of the amalgam of error for magnetic direction finding, it remains dependable. Once the human energy to provide for and update deviation and variation errors has been expended, a compass will tell us something approximating the truth, and will continue to do so dependably and cheaply.

In navigation a compass course should rarely be depended upon for more than 24 hours and, ideally for as little as one or two if you find yourself in waters that display interesting currents such as the Gulf Stream. The sophisticated navigator compares the compass reading with the sun's reading at least once a day. A compass works superbly well in the short run, which is all we need to get about the globe and, anyway, as a professor of mine once observed, "In the long run we are all dead."

Learn to trust your compass but only in the short run. That far it will serve you well. But never forget the first law of magnetic navigation, "Eternal vigilance is the price of true north."

"4.51 A magnetic anomaly was reported in July 1965 by HMS Falmouth whilst on passage between positions in approximately 23° N, 37° E and 22 ° N, 37.5° E."

I'd never seen a magnetic anomaly and hoped to never see one. But if I ever did, I hoped that it would be someplace other than in that navigator's nightmare, the Red Sea. And in the Red Sea anyplace would be better than a few miles west of Shi'b Shu'aiba, a nasty reef just off the coast of inhospitable Saudi Arabia.

There was no suggestion on the charts that there might be a navigational problem in the area. The only hint of trouble was the easily missed, offhand reference to a possibility that appeared in the British Red Sea Pilot in 1965 and was never mentioned again. Nor was there any mention of the extent of the error nor of the potential for disaster.

Had the anomaly been one that led the sailor, unknowing but fail-safe away from the reefs, the lack of references might have been condoned but the anomaly rediscovered on my sailing vessel *Unlikely* on 19 December 1984 put any northbound vessel in serious jeopardy.

On the Red Sea leg of our circumnavigation we found ourselves at 23°10' N and 37°20' E. We were sailing a course of 340° and in the course of three hours our SatNav informed us that we were being set towards east by 15°. It was night and overcast and we were being set inexorably and mysteriously toward the reefs.

We kicked our course to 325° and three hours later according to SatNav we were still 15° in error. Since no eddy is that powerful or that consistent we abandoned the chart and checked into the pilot. It was then, after missing it at first, that we dug out the hidden, tiny type paragraph reprinted above.

We had stumbled across a little known and highly dangerous magnetic anomaly. It is a doubly dangerous condition because of its proximity to dangerous reefs and because the misinformation that it generated turns boats toward, not away from, the reefs. We tracked it up the 37° longitude line until it started to weaken at 24°18' and had quite dissipated by 24°35'.

The anomaly is still unincorporated into the charts. Just like the ship wreckers of Devon and Cornwall who moved lights around onshore to misguide luckless sailors, it silently and insidiously beckons mariners to the reefs of Arabia.

Your charts are your salvation. They have more information on them than you will ever need and everything means something. They are almost without fail correct. Doubt your wife, doubt your sanity, if you must, but doubt your charts only after checking, rechecking and deeply pondering something that does not look right. In thirty years at sea I only found one dangerous error and that was an error of omission, not of commission.

There are many bad places to be at sea. Many can be avoided if you plan your passage responsibly. Those that come upon you unexpectedly usually will not kill you but often make you wish you were dead.

One of these places is the Red Sea beset not only by storms and reefs but by folk along its shores whose hatred is just as palpable as a jagged reef. Another is our own Cape Hatteras where the Gulf Stream rushes up to meet the cold air off the North Atlantic.

But, for my money, the worst, because it is the least anticipated, is that much overrated, overpublicized and overlied about Mediterranean. If you would believe the Greeks, bearing the gifts of the Med, the sailing is sun drenched and idyllic. Sailboats get wafted by pleasant breezes from one delicious and friendly port to the next.

Sun drenched . . . yes, when not rain drenched. Idyllic . . . mostly when reading the idylls of Hellenic heroes. And when it comes to pleasant breezes, better you should be just south of Cape Horn.

My wife and I and a young couple escaping from the dreadful rigors of Romania rounded the headlands leading up towards Piraeus. We saluted the great temple to Poseidon that rules over his domain from the heights of a great cape. The winds were reasonable and the seas acceptable.

Things got quickly worse as the wind shifted from the east as a meltemi roared down from the mountains of Greece. We could make no way northward and the motion became so rough that the poor Romanians, so full of hope and joy in escaping from Romania, huddled on the cockpit floor in terror. They yearned loudly to be back in Bucharest.

There was no letup and we had to escape from the bitter north wind. A hasty glance at the chart showed an island, Sérifos, only an hour's sail to starboard. On the island we caught the name of a harbor, Livadhi. We consulted the cruising pilot and found that Livadhi was "a large, pleasant and roomy harbor, with good facilities and especially well protected from the winds from the north."

Wow! Just what we needed and off we went, lickety split on a wild reach for the harbor entrance. The entrance was a little rough with seas rolling across it but it was, as always in any storm, infinitely inviting.

We roared in and found ourselves not in a pleasant and protected harbor but in a small pool, a couple of hundred yards across, dotted with abandoned and rusted iron coaling structures. The seas rolling in from the entrance were breaking along the shore at the back of the harbor only a few boat lengths away.

Where was the pleasant refuge we had expected? How could both the chart and the pilot be so wrong? Unable to stay in the small and dangerous place we fought our way out over the incoming seas and winds and, reasoning that the other side might give a little protection we rounded the southern cape.

It was like crossing the narrow line between heaven and hell. The seas flattened, the winds abated, and the Romanians raised their heads. As we sailed up the protected coast a lovely harbor entrance opened. The harbor itself was all that any sailor could ever pray for. No seas, no winds, plenty of room, no iron coaling wreckages and nifty people.

As we tied up to a well protected pier assisted by helpful fishermen we called out,

"What harbor is this?"

"Why, this is the harbor of Livadhi," they answered.

"What do you mean, Livadhi? We just pulled into Livadhi, a terrible place on the other side of the island. If this is Livadhi, what is the other place?"

"Oh", came the reply, "that is the *other* Livadhi."

We rushed to the chart and sure enough upon close scrutiny with a magnifying glass we found that there were two separate harbors, one on the east side and one on the west side of Sérifos with the same latitude and longitude, give or take half a minute, and with exactly the same name.

Unexpected? You bet. But that is the moral of this story. At sea, always and forever expect the unexpected and always and forever trust your charts.

NAVIGATION HARDWARE

The Sextant

The sun is a great big thing and hard to miss. Since you will not be seeking excruciating accuracy far at sea, your affordable plastic sextant will tell you approximately where you are as well as an expensive Plath. It is not the equipment that will be found wanting, it will be you, whose margin for error in taking in the sights will be much larger than the accuracy difference between the dearest and the cheapest sextants you can buy. The only thing really wrong with a plastic sextant is that it doesn't make you *feel* like a navigator. People tend to snicker and your crew will begin to look a bit worried. So maybe you ought to spend a few hundred bucks on a better one.

The Dividers

It is O.K. to buy the cheapest sextant, but it is imperative that you get the most expensive pair of dividers that you can find. The best are still made in Merrie Olde England and the best of them are the single-handed kind that you can open or close with one hand. The heavier they are the easier they will be to use. Keep in mind that you will probably be sick, tired, and scared when they will be needed most, so get something with a heft, something that reassures and sets down hard, rather than some fluffy little pair that skitters about. Be sure to keep the pointy ends sharp.

The Parallel Rules

Let your parallel rules be as transparent as your ignorance of celestial navigation. I cannot imagine anyone using a pair of rules that you cannot see through. Beware of the beveled edges since a beveled edge refracts the lines beneath to places they should not be.

The Handbearing Compass

You will need a handbearing compass like the French Mini. Night lighted by some kind of nuclear magic, self damping and free of parallax and batteries, it is a welcome relief from what you had to put up with a few years ago. It comes built into a rubber ring and is amenable to a bit of rough and tumble. More up to date are the electronic hand helds which are really nifty. How they work, I do not have the foggiest; however, they do work until a nasty sea comes aboard and zaps their innards.

The Binoculars

The slickest, costliest, and most honored brands among marine optics generally do a lousy job. Not even a lousy job for the money, just a plain lousy job. Many are burdened with a ridiculous little internal compass optically coupled to the magnification capability and adding little more than confusion and cost. All the most expensive binoculars are center focusing, which means than neither eye is ever in focus. Some even have a zoom feature, the use of which escapes me.

The binoculars to buy are the wide-angle, 7 x 50 power cheap binoculars. These are optically adequate, have blessed individual focusing for each eye, and can often boast a wider field of vision than the megabuck zoomers. However, the salt water does get inside them, and you can only get about a year out of a pair before they go dim. The salt water gets into the expensive models, too, and just as quickly.

The Log

You will need some method of determining how fast you are going through the water. Combined with your compass, this will allow you a dead reckoning check of your celestial fixes. Absent all else, tie a knot in one end of a hundred feet of light line and hang a drogue (a small funnel) on the other end. Let the line run out till you feel the knot. Time the running out. If it takes 60 seconds you are doing one knot, 30 seconds two knots, 20 seconds three knots, 15 seconds four knots, 12 seconds five knots, and 10 seconds six knots. This is a chip log and will accurately replace an expensive electronics piece.

YOUR ELECTRONIC NAVIGATION OPTIONS

Your Yankee ingenuity goes out the window when electrons rush in the front door. In the world of whirly ions no one can be self-reliant. We all are at the mercy of unknowable electronic technology. Since the passagemaking sailor must never be lured too far away from self-reliance, any involvement in electronics must be very cautiously assessed.

The electronic options for sailors outlined here are all based on our inability to effect repairs at sea, and on the known intransigence and failure rates of electronic devices. Only when you accept these two conditions, unrepairability and intransigence, can you afford to play about with electronics.

The First Option: Do Without

Simply do without any electronics. There are plenty of backup systems that can efficiently replace all but one of the electronic marine marvels. It is quite possible, nay even quite pleasant and rewarding, to substitute the inside of your head, which you can control, for the inside of a black box that you cannot. If you cannot fix something with the equivalent of beating it with a stick, go back to the systems that you can.

The only two pieces of electronic gear of which I would be sad to be deprived, and for which there are no satisfactory mechanical substitutes, are a depthfinder and an RDF. The most reliable, and cheapest, fathometer is the one with a revolving disc and little red flashing lights that indicate the depth by the distance between the lights on the disc. In theory, and in execution, it is steam engine simple. I have repaired mine several times onboard.

Also consider Speedtech's newly developed, waterproof, handheld, cheap, battery operated fathometer which looks like a flashlight and works like a dream. It is a great back up for a fixed fathometer and the only way, short of throwing a lead line, that I know for finding, from your dinghy, an unmarked entrance across a strange reef.

The Second Option: The Lowest High-Tech

Should you have an irresistible compulsion for electronics, never go with the latest state-of-the-art version. As far as I have been able to determine, state-of-the-art means that the manufacturers overcharge you for something that will be a tenth of the price in two years. The best electronics are the previous generation of electronics. They have been around long enough to have been weaned from their most arrogant faults and, since they are now old fashioned, usually by a matter of some months, they are closeout cheap.

The Third Option: The Whole Electronic Hog

There is an ineffable and, to some, an irresistible charm about the very latest, up-to-the-second, state-of-the-art model of anything. In spite of all the urging in this book for simplicity, I confess to a secret, almost immoral passion for what the newest of those damn black boxes can do. They seem to have the final answers. They encourage our insatiable itch to know it all. For those of you who share that attraction with me, then go the whole hog.

"All" today means the integration of every one of your ship's systems into an onboard computer that will sense trouble, correct errors, avoid collisions, warn of shallows, navigate, pilot, and direct your little vessel safely to harbor by referring to digitized marine charts—reduced to a few small diskettes— any of which can instantly be called up on your screen. These new, integrated, computerized systems confer on skippers a sense of godlike power and control, at least till they blow. For those sailors whose boats are already in perfect shape, and who have little else left to work on, or to pay for, the new instruments provide an endless and fascinating game of keeping them humming, buzzing, flashing, and gurgling.

On a small sailing vessel, where space and money and energy are all at a premium, and where our *raison d'être* is to simplify our lives, the electronic options must remain just that, options only. They must be backed up with tough, reliable, and unutterably simple systems for that inevitable moment when all electronics fail from inherent complication or the demise of shipboard electricity. Electronics must remain a game for the sophisticated passagemaker but, after all, no one wants to be serious all the time.

Play the expensive electronic pin-ball game if you can afford it, but never allow the cost of what is only a game preclude you from your passages.

CHAPTER 7

Communications

SEA COMMUNICATIONS

One of the larger fears that beset those about to take to the deep seas for the first time is the possibility of not being able to call for aid and succor, or not being able to just talk with other folk. Paradoxically, after we do get to sea, we find that the isolation itself becomes a wonderful experience, something to be wished for, not dreaded. Enforced aloneness often reveals an inner trip to the fantasy castles of our own mind, with higher turrets and towers than Walt ever dreamed of.

It is perfectly rational to worry about being in danger and having no reasonably available aid. The other fear, separation from our own kind, is no less rational for not being based on a physical threat. So, to urge you offshore there must be available a way for you to seek aid when in sailorly trouble, and to seek contact with another human voice if only to satisfy the ancient need to gather, as it were, around the campfire at the end of the day.

I have only twice in 30 years of passaging had to resort to a call for emergency assistance, but often when I am at sea I feel the need to hear another voice. Even though I compulsively yatter at sea, I have remained sufficiently unsocial to enjoy the option of merely flipping a switch when I tire of contact. I can then climb back inside my own head.

Communication at sea, whether it be to seek aid when in danger or to soothe our ineffable loneliness, faces obstacles.

Weather, distance, and even sunspots contribute to the difficulty of making yourself understood. If you are speaking with the crew of another small sailboat, they are as tired, harried, and may even be as seasick as you. The act of communicating, which on land merely involves the opening of the mouth, at sea becomes an exhausting activity.

Because it is such a drain on your limited energies, sea communications must be accomplished quickly, clearly, and with as little effort as possible. A simple five-minute phone call on land may require, at sea, a whole evening of intense concentration. As a result of these difficulties, techniques for passing along information have developed that lend precision to a tedious art.

THE ESPERANTO OF THE SEA

Most human conversations are held between you and the other guy standing toe-to-toe and nose-to-nose. Acquired tricks for making sure that you understand each other are marshalled for even the most simple transfer of intelligence. The sounds coming from your mouth, the expressions on your face, the language of your body and hands, and an occasional quick sketch on the tablecloth, are all needed to even approximate mutual understanding. Alas, sometimes all of this does not help, even though you are looking your counterpart right in the eye. The transfer of understanding, even *tête-à-tête*, is a very tricky business. Ask any high school teacher.

Between vessels at sea there is no *tête* to *tête*. Conversation is aways at a distance, and what you are trying to say is usually filtered through winds that shove your words down your throat and seas that make concentration nigh impossible. Until Marconi came along all communication at sea dealt in human distances, how far the sailor could see and hear. Radio was really no revolution, it simply extended the distances, and since it lacks the face-to-face assists to which we are accustomed in wrenching understanding from each other, the use of wireless requires special care.

Since communication without understanding is about as useful as a soft bridegroom, sailors have long sought a method, a shorthand, that could guarantee understanding under obstructive conditions. As we shall see, they have been pretty successful. Maybe we ought to teach it to the politicians.

The obvious need was to construct a language that would excise the devious content of normal communication. The new language had to be characterized by three elements: clarity, conciseness, and universality. The crucial nature of emergencies at sea demands that the intelligence transmitted be *clear*, that is, readable to both sender and receiver. The tiny windows of opportunity that exist for most transmissions at sea demanded *conciseness*, that is, short and to the point, and the language had to be *universal*.

Such a mariner's language was devised and accepted around the middle of the nineteenth century. It has been honed and refined for the past hundred years, surviving the coming of both the aviation and the nuclear ages. The language, for it is nothing else, is a collection of messages identified by one or two of the 26 letters of our alphabet, sometimes modified by a single-digit numeral.

Signals are rarely more than two letters in length. Every two-letter signal has exactly the same prescribed meaning in any language and under any circumstance. The entire language, and every piece of meaning that it encompasses, is contained in a slim and wonderful volume bearing the curious name of *International Code of Signals*. It is, bar none, the most fascinating book on the sea for the serious offshore sailor.

Merely a careful reading of the *International Code of Signals* will give insight into the nature of sea emergencies and the ancient responses that sailors have evolved. It is the irreplaceable primer for understanding how to act in difficulties and it gives the reader, newly come to the sea, a grasp of how rescuers will respond to appeals, what rescuers need in the way of information, and what assistance they expect from the vessel in difficulty.

Until the coming of radio, this "Sea Esperanto" required only the knowledge of the alphabet and the alphabet flags that represent each letter. Radio communication introduced the need for the Morse code, since voice transmission by radio is infinitely less dependable than the clear, strong dots and dashes of continuous wave (CW) transmission. So learn a little Morse.

Read carefully this charming little volume. Read it and you will know as much as any admiral about communicating at sea.

Until the beginning of this century, communications between ships at sea was carried on primarily by signal flags. With Marconi's discovery, the importance of flags declined to the point that few sailors today have any knowledge of them. However, even without formal knowledge of the language of flags, we still, almost without realizing, do lots of flag signaling. All of us know that a white flag signals a desire to surrender. We know that a red flag in the water with a diagonal stripe signals a diver down and a U.S. flag flown upside down is a signal of distress. Skull and crossbones are for pirates and a cocktail glass on any color background is an invite to imbibe. The ubiquitous circle crossed by a diagonal forbids everything from smoking to shoes aboard and all of us are aware that a yellow flag signals quarantine and a desire to talk to officials.

Notwithstanding easy radio communication between an entering ship and the officials ashore, it is still necessary to fly your own flag as well as a courtesy flag of the country that you are entering and thereby hangs a lovely tale.

We were entering English Harbour, Antigua, after a transatlantic passage and found, to our dismay, that we had blown to shreds all of our Stars and Stripes. Antigua has a reputation for being a stickler for protocol and there was no way that we could enter flagless. As we were about to try the difficult task of drawing a U.S. pennant (think of all those stars), my wife, with a joyous Ta Da!, pulled a plastic bag used by the Fawcett store in Annapolis. It is a large bag with a beautiful diagonally flowing Stars and Stripes printed on both sides. We hastily taped a piece of cardboard inside and ran it up. No official had any objection and we subsequently mailed it to Fawcett's with a "thank you" for the assist. Fawcett framed and mounted the flag-bag with our letter and, as far as I know, it is still somewhere displayed in the shop.

On another occasion we were beating up the troublesome Gulf of Suez which had Egyptian soldiers posted on either bank along with other armed folk dissatisfied with the U.S. policy of the moment. Our U.S. flag attracted much attention and not a few rifle shots. It was impossible to sail without a flag since we would have been stopped and boarded and it would have been most embarrassing, and totally illegal, to hide behind the flag of a different country. What to do?

As I rummaged in my flag inventory I spotted a large flag of the Confederate States of America. We ran it up, hoping that it was close enough to the U.S. pennant to avoid the charge of deceit and yet far enough from the real Stars and Stripes to confuse the hell out of the shooters. It worked like a charm and for the rest of that difficult passage not only were we not shot at along the shore, but we received salutes, rebel yells and hoorays, and on one occasion some ice cream from the everpresent Texans working the oil rigs we passed.

RADIO COMMUNICATIONS AT SEA

We sail off to sea in our little vessels that sibilantly whisper away a thousand miles and then, somehow, suddenly, we are hungry for noises louder and less familiar than the beating of our own hearts. We are lonesome for the cacophony of humankind.

There are three types of radio communication available to the offshore sailor: Very high frequency (VHF), high frequency marine single sideband (SSB), and amateur or ham radio, which includes both VHF and SSB. Each has its own uses, and while they are somewhat interchangeable, none does exactly the job of the other.

Very High Frequency VHF (Marine VHF)

Range. Mostly within line of sight and rarely more than about 25 miles.

Uses. For close communication with ships at sea, for contact with on-land VHF stations such as the Coast Guard, and for contacting port captains as you close land.

Emergency Uses. Of very little use at sea and only limited usefulness longshore. Very useful in harbor.

Expertise Required. None. Pick up the microphone, push the button, and you are on the air.

Installation. Dead easy to install. Comes with a matched antenna that needs very little grounding, and the 25-watt output is more power than you will ever require.

Deficiencies. Short range, and usually there is no one about to chat with.

Cost. Not expensive these days, and the installation is easy. Incidentally, do not buy the fancy expensive sets with "bells and whistles." All Marine VHF have the same FCC required minimum and maximum capabilities.

Marine Single Sideband HF
(Commercial Single Sideband, SSB)

Range. Worldwide. You are in communication with powerful and expensive commercial land stations.

Uses. Primarily useful for business and commercial communication. This is the only long distance service on which you can "do a deal."

Emergency Uses. Very useful for short-term immediate response. Not very good for long-term difficulties and long-term monitoring.

Expertise Required. None. Everything is pre-set and pre-crystaled to commercial channels. Because the land stations are extremely powerful, you will always hear them and they mostly will always hear you. Most of the time it is just "push to talk."

Installation. Since no expertise is required of the user, much is required of the installer. The installation should be done by the vendor. With luck the installation will be O.K.

Deficiencies. The chief problem is expense, but SSB is also awkward for obtaining precious information from other small vessels. Few passaging sailboats have commercial SSB. It is mostly used by big power megayachts to whom you have as little to say as they to you.

Cost. SSB is costly to buy, costly to install, costly to use, and costly to maintain. Every contact you make is a long-distance overseas charge call, and your bill can easily add up to kilo bucks.

Amateur Radio Service
(Ham Radio, VHF and HF Single Sideband)

Range. Worldwide, around the corner, and everywhere in between. There are few places on the globe that you cannot reach at some hour of the day. The range is affected by daylight/darkness variations, sunspot activity, and other mysterious impediments to propagation, but you can always talk to someone, somewhere.

Uses. Covers every conceivable use that might arise on a small sailing vessel. There is always a ham listening somewhere in the world. A call to any U.S. ham can be patched into the U.S. telephone system and all you pay for is from his home to the home of the person called. Ham radio at sea provides regular nets who update weather information over the precise waters in which you may be sailing. There are medical nets that provide emergency advice and long-term monitoring of an injury or illness. Technical nets will help you solve mechanical problems.

Ham radio has its own VHF frequencies on which local hams get together via repeater stations in almost any city or port you will visit. As an amateur, you will be able to enter into the life of any new country via a host of new and helpful friends.

Emergency Uses. Ham radio is the most effective method of reaching professional (read Coast Guard) help when you are *really* in trouble. Your call may travel half around the world to alert rescuers ten miles from your position, but the ubiquity of hams and their desire to be of assistance is as useful as a liferaft. Any Mayday call will be instantly acknowledged, and the frequency will be cleared all over the world and guarded for your use alone for so long as your emergency lasts. Foolish is the passagemaker who is not a ham.

Expertise Required. Aye, there's the rub. You do have to know something about radio. The need for technical knowledge is the other side of the coin of the enormous range of use provided by ham radio. Since there is so much that can be done, and so many places on the bands to do it, easy automatic operation is not built in. You need a license to operate, for which you must pass tests covering some knowledge of radio and some facility with the Morse code. Since Morse relates to many other methods of communication at sea (flags, RDF, light, Navlights, and sound), it behooves you to know Morse anyway. It will take you about three months of light study (an hour a day) to pass the test. Any ham club has classes and will be delighted to help.

Installation. You will learn enough in your ham classes to do your own installation. Find a ham sailor, buy him a case of beer, and he will work his heart out with you on the installation. Read the manuals.

Deficiencies. Ham radio is subject to the same problems of dependability and repairability endemic to all electronics but, due to your training and studies, most problems can be dealt with by you or by the more expert ham on the next boat. If you have problems at sea that are beyond your capability, wait until the next port where there will be a ham with a soldering iron eager to be of assistance.

Cost. A good, used, state-of-the-art station can be put together for under a thousand dollars, an all-new station for not much more than two thousand. Divide that by the free phone calls, information networks, and the emergency uses of ham radio, and the cost is zilch. Get a ham license.

AMATEUR RADIO NETS

Amateur radio nets are run by people who do it for the love of it. They are unpaid, self-taught, and trained. The nets are basically only regulated by themselves. Amateur radio is an argument for anarchy. Paradoxically, the hams themselves are the most law-abiding and considerate of folk.

The nets have fixed frequencies that are held at fixed times. Most of the important nets are daily and cover some portion of the 24 hours on a given frequency. Some frequencies, like the very important 14.313 MHz, have been reserved (unofficially, but all abide by the reservation) for exclusive maritime use. This frequency is in operation 24 hours a day with different volunteer net controllers taking different segments of the time. It is an exhausting job to keep communications going, sometimes under difficult conditions of propagation. The controllers have become extremely proficient at handling traffic and remain constantly attuned to the possibility of an emergency call.

Here is how a net works. The controller will come on at the beginning of the net and identify the net and himself by a call sign. The controller will then call for any emergency, medical, or "good and welfare" messages (all considered "priority traffic") and these will be handled first. Should a real emergency arise at any time during the net, Mayday! Mayday!, the frequency will be cleared and kept clear for the exclusive use of the vessel calling for aid.

After priority traffic has been dealt with, other stations waiting to pass traffic will check in with their call signs and await their turn till the controller calls them into the net.

When a station comes into the net it usually does so by calling another ham station. The call (CQ in amateur lingo) will be transmitted, and if the other station is present on the frequency, the two stations will go off net frequency so as not to interfere with the continuing process of linking up.

The nets exist primarily to effect these linkages. They provide a common meeting ground for amateur sailors who will listen each day for any traffic that might be directed at them. When you go to sea you have a million hams to look after you. Get a ham ticket and tune them in. Like Shmoos, they love to be used.

CHAPTER 8

Minimal Mechanics

An expert is a fool with a beard from another city.

ANONYMOUS

INSPECTION-MAINTENANCE-REDUNDANCY-REPAIR-DO WITHOUT

Of all the problems that you will have to overcome, mechanical failure should be the last to keep you from the far horizons. Any passage can be completed without an engine, without electricity, with a leaky boat and a jury-rigged mast. And you can certainly do without your electronics.

To go offshore you only need know what will get you back to port. Nowhere is this premise more useful than with machinery. If you wait until you are a master mechanic you will never get to sea. You only need to be able to finish your passage should some, most or all machinery go belly-up.

An offshore sailor must develop a disciplined approach to keeping things going:

Inspection must be daily, immediately followed by

Maintenance for any problems turned up by inspection, and for the prevention of future problems. For those problems not amenable to maintenance, the next step is

Redundance, which means replacement or backup of the faulty equipment or system. If this is not successful the offshore sailor attempts

Repair at sea. Should this be unsuccessful, the prudent passagemaker must be psychologically prepared to

Do Without.

Inspection

DECK LEVEL

Start aft at the centerline and work forward along the starboard side and back aft along the port. Observe the following:

Steering. Check the sheaves and cables for looseness or wear. Check the rudder-post quadrant and wheel gears. Check the wheel for play.

Self-steering. Check the windvane for loose nuts and general condition. Check the autopilot mounting and check for signs of overheating.

Backstay. Check the swages for cracks, and the turnbuckles for distortion or signs of loosening. Check the turnbuckle locking device.

Winches. Check for binding.

Sheets. Check for wear or chafe.

Shrouds. Same as the backstay.

Deck Fittings. Check for corrosion, general condition, and signs of wear or binding.

Deck Cargo. Carefully check all fastenings each morning for looseness, wear, or chafe. Check the liferaft.

Anchors. Check the lashings.

Headstay. Same as the backstay.

Mast. Check the base for movement and leakage. Check the mast for tuning.

Sails and Halyards. Check the sails for signs of chafe or weakened seams. Check the halyards, by feel and by binoculars, for attachment problems at the head, foot, and clew.

Instruments. Check operation of all deck-mounted instruments.

General. Check for the presence of all deck equipment such as lifevests, winch handles, flashlights, man-overboard pole, liferings, etc. (Prepare an equipment checklist for this inspection.)

BELOW DECKS

Check all fittings, tubes, hoses, and electrical connections. Check for above-waterline leaks. Check the stove and gas fittings. Check the waterpumps. Check all instruments below for operation.

Check the galley and the heads for cleanliness, and carefully check the heads for blockage and operation. Check the forepeak for leaks and the chain locker for tangled or shifted chain. Check the food and water stores for spoilage or damage.

BILGE

Open all floorboards and climb into the bilge. Check the operation of both manual and electric bilge pumps. *Observe for oil leaks.* Look at, smell, and taste bilge water. Check drive belts for signs of wear or looseness. Check all tube, pipe, and hose connections for leaks or signs of wear. Check the battery fastenings and connections for looseness and corrosion.

Check Oil. Check the battery water level. Visually check fuel oil filters. Stay in the bilge for a while and think about things.

Maintenance

There are two levels of maintenance: scheduled maintenance, required by the equipment manuals, and emergency maintenance, dictated by the appearance of problems.

A scheduled maintenance log should be prepared and maintenance should be undertaken, if necessary, according to manufacturer's recommendations. Emergency maintenance is mostly a matter of tightening nuts, lubrication, and attention to chafe and wear conditions.

Redundance

Redundance assumes that if something breaks you'll use something else. Redundance can be replacing an entire piece of equipment, or replacing the function of the failed equipment with a backup system. A redundant system for a failed electric waterpump, for example, is a hand pump. A redundant system for a failed GPS can be another GPS (equipment replacement) or reversion to the sextant (function replacement).

Repair at Sea

Most things are temporarily repairable using bailing wire, band-aids, dental floss, and prayer. When you get into port there will be time enough to get more sophisticated and expensive assistance. The engineering on a modern boat is not entirely unsophisticated, but a lot of stuff can be done at sea.

Do Without

Even when all mechanical equipment has failed there still is the ultimate backup of your sails. If you can keep your hull afloat—

sailboats are surprisingly hard to sink—you will eventually come ashore somewhere.

DIESELS, ELECTRICS, AND LEAKS

How to Keep Things under Control till You Reach Port

Other than your sails, there are three mechanical systems that are really nice to have in working order on an offshore passage: your power plant to push you along, your electrics, the source of so much comfort en route, and the integrity of your hull, without which all else doesn't matter much.

To keep these three systems operating for the 30 days or so that you are out of sight of land requires little expertise but does need a whole bucket of guts and self-confidence. Without much knowledge, most things mechanical can be made to hobble along for a month, but *sans* belief in your own capabilities, admittedly limited, the hobbling comes to a halt.

Of the three systems only hull integrity is crucial. You can go anywhere in the world with a broken engine and empty batteries but you won't get a yard and a half with a bad leak. All three systems are easily dealt with, even the leaks, and the "fear of fixing" any of them should not keep you home. Nothing should keep you home.

How Even You Can Fix Your Diesel

There are three diesel sounds with which you must become familiar, characteristic *voices* to which you must hearken. The first is your engine's remarkably constant, healthy voice. This

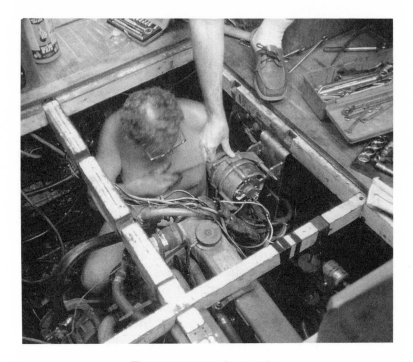

The proper place for a sailor.

may vary a bit with the boat's motion in heavy seas, but when it alters significantly, look for trouble. The other two are the troublesome voices, one a bit faster and the other a bit slower than normal. Both will appear just before the engine quits. If your diesel speeds up it is a minute away from running out of fuel. If it slows down it is either too hot or out of lubricating oil. Both give you a few seconds to shut down before it gets complicated.

We were again in the Red Sea, which seems ever to test a sailor's mettle. I was sound asleep as we started to beat into the wind toward Hurghada. The night had been very hot and draining with the wind from aft and the head wind, although still warm, had a refreshing draft to it.

Something woke me, an indefinable sense of not exactly something wrong but certainly something not just exactly right. I lay abunk for a while wondering what could have pulled me from so exhausted a sleep. I called up to the watch and was assured that all was well. I listened to the wind which carried no tale of distress and I listened to the reassuring creaking of the hull and the click of the little creatures in the water as we rushed past them.

I listened to the engine.

It seemed just the slightest bit quieter than usual. I assumed that my still drugged state accounted for that, but, urged by the gentler than usual purring of the engine, I developed an unscratchable itch to look in the bilge where the engine was purring away.

Tired and unalarmed I almost dozed off again. Luckily duty and guilt called more loudly than sleep and I rolled out of my bunk and pulled the floorboards up. What I saw will stay with me the rest of my life.

The bilge in which the engine lay is about five feet deep. The bilge was filled to just below the air intake of the diesel, covering and quieting the sounds of propulsion. It was this quieting that called me to the engine and a few seconds more we would have had salt water in the air intake.

I was convinced that we were sinking and since the automatic bilgepump had failed (and was, anyway, inadequate) all hands were called to bucket duty at 4 A.M. After half an hour, and to our enormous relief, the level started to fall and the voice of my engine returned to normal.

What happened was that as we sailed on a following wind the ports in the fo'c'sle had been opened for a breath of air. When the wind shifted ahead and we began a beat, the seas quietly entered the open ports and filled our bilge.

Listen well to the voice of your engine. Like the voice of the turtle, it is subtle and quiet but carries news of great import.

What you need to know about repairing your diesel is only what will get you into the harbor. There are only six problems, all of which you can correct at sea, that could cause your engine to go suddenly from O.K. to stop. Other than these six, you would probably have to hit it repeatedly with a maul to induce a failure:

Salt water up the tail pipe.

Lack of air.

Loss of lubricating oil.

Malfunctioning waterpump.

Adulterated fuel.

Lack of fuel.

SALT WATER UP THE TAIL PIPE

Loop your exhaust pipe to the masthead if you can. Loop it high and often and do not put too much faith in patented fancy exhaust systems. A loop is wonderful and cheap and effective, as long as you remember to install that little anti-siphoning valve at its very top and check it now and then.

LACK OF AIR

Every engine room is, or should be, supplied with a vent that exits on deck. Should your engine stop, check that vent first—someone is always sleeping over mine with blankets and foul-weather gear plugging the vent—although your engine probably has a dozen alternate ways of getting air. Much more likely is a blockage in the air intake at the top of the engine. Some engines have an oil blowback fed into the air intake that often clogs the air filter.

LOSS OF LUBRICATING OIL

This is the chief disaster that can happen to your engine. Unless caught before you run dry, you are stuck with a pure sailboat for the rest of your passage and a large bill at the end of it. A little device can be wired into your oil-pressure gauge to automatically kill your engine should pressure fall below a safe level. We built our own out of a relay and an oil-pressure sensing device. These devices can be had commercially; it is a foolhardy act to sail without them.

MALFUNCTIONING WATERPUMPS

The heart of that great, strong chunk of hardened steel called your engine is a small, soft piece of rubber. This is the water-pump impeller that keeps the coolant moving, without which nothing else will move at all. It is easy to install and should be the first place that you look (after you check the waterpump belt) in the event of a temperature rise. Carry spare belts and spare impellers. No problem. Make sure there are no leaks in your water lines and that your salt water intake is not clogged.

ADULTERATED FUEL

The flow of fuel is most often interrupted by inadequate filtering. The best advice I ever got was, "install filters till you feel silly and then install just as many more."

Most fuel filtration systems have see-through glass cups so you have no excuse for not checking frequently. Even if they look clean, whip them off and wipe them out. You will be glad you did.

In the U.S. fuel is not often intentionally laced with water. In the Third World, where you are most likely to be sailing, a gallon of fuel represents a day's pay, and water, which is usually polluted and dirty, is free. As a result, vendors often stretch their profits by adding water. Abroad you are also likely to get your oil in old fuel drums from which you must *never* pump the bottom six inches directly into your tanks. The bottom of the barrel is where the water lies and it is where the dirt gathers.

Filter suspect fuel through a fine mesh screen funnel during fueling. Put fuel additive such as Biobor JF in the fuel to kill the algae that grow in diesel fuel.

LACK OF FUEL

Forgetting to switch tanks is a frequent cause of engine stoppage. I will not comment on this, not because such an oversight is beneath my contempt, but because I have done just that too many times myself. Interruption of the fuel supply introduces air into the system which then must be bled. Newer engines bleed themselves. Learn how to bleed.

Should this embarrassment happen, bleed your engine of air to get it going again. It is an uncomfortable job at sea but not a difficult one if you have had the foresight to practice before leaving harbor. Trying to bleed your engine for the first time in a dark bilge, in a bad seaway, tired and a little scared, with the engine manual in one hand and wrenches in the other, is high up on my list of stuff I would rather not do. With practice, however, it is a cinch even in the dark.

GETTING IT GOING AGAIN

There are many scenarios for restarting an engine with flat batteries. By hand is best, but the least likely to be successful, given the unnecessarily large engines we lug around. Keeping a separate battery charged and out of the starting circuit is certainly prudent. Dry battery packs, alleged to deliver 25 amps, are available, but they are dangerous to depend upon.

For those of us who failed to install backup batteries and cannot hand start, there is one method of restarting in the absence of electrical power that requires no additional equipment. It is rarely referred to but is so sensible that you must, at the very least, attempt it before setting sail. It uses the torque of your propeller while under way.

Try doing this one day before you set out on your long passage:

Put transmission in neutral.

Release your propeller brake.

Engage the compression valves on all cylinders.

Release the belts to the alternators, generator, starter motor, waterpump, and any other hindrances that might add a drag to your engine but are not required for the engine to start.

Bring the boat up to hull speed on a broad reach.

Ease into forward gear.

When and if the spinning propeller commences to turn the engine over, flip the compression valve down on one cylinder, advance the throttle, and the engine should start. Then sequentially flip down all the rest. If it starts, let it warm up, stop it, belt the waterpump back on, and repeat the whole thing. Then stop it again, do the same for one alternator, and you are back in business.

I say "if" and "should" because your engine may be too heavy to be turned by your propeller, or it may not have the proper reduction gear for this maneuver. When it does work it is the quintessential backup for dead batteries on a sailboat.

Waltzing With Your Electrics

Three quarters of the time marine electrical equipment does not work well and the other quarter it does not work at all. It is not entirely the fault of the equipment. The problem is that your friendly boatbuilder electricians think that an alternator is some sort of sexual deviant. The best thing to do with a new boat is what I did after we were nearly electrocuted by life lines (!) that were neatly grounded into the 110-volt shorepower circuit. I tore everything out and rewired the whole boat. This is a good move even if the life lines are not hot. Problems that generally result from wear and tear are amenable to regular maintenance and easy repair. In electrical systems the real problem is to find the fault.

FAULTY CONNECTIONS

No matter what the electrical problem is, the first thing to look for is an interruption in the circuit. Your boat is in such constant motion and in such a lousy, wet, and salty atmosphere that it is to be expected that connections will fail. Marine electrical systems prove the Russian adage, "It is no wonder that the bear dances well, but that he dances at all."

Wire-to-wire joinings at dry points below deck must be soldered. Those subjected to salt water are best joined by careful crimping.

There is no substitute for melting things together on a boat. If you could fuse the whole electrical system into one continuous, unbroken, solid circuit not subject to salt, half the electrical problems would disappear. That is exactly what is done in those little integrated circuits in your electronics. Problems of discontinuity are easily handled at sea with a small, inexpensive voltmeter and a lot of patience. In the presence of sea water, even connections that look good, especially soldered connections, can be corroded and offer too much resistance to the flow of current. In the event of electrical failure, check every wire, especially that little bugger way down under the fridge. The harder they are to get at the sooner they fail. That is an immutable law of the sea.

ALTERNATORS

Do not depend on those minuscule auto alternators that allegedly deliver 50 amps; 120 amps will keep you warm, happy, and visible.

If an alternator blows either replace it with a spare or do without. If you must do without it is no big deal. Use dry cells or kerosene for light below, hand steer or use a windvane, transmit radio signals only in an emergency, and use the previously installed (I certainly hope) hand pumps in your galley and head. This should give you plenty of reserve, emergency power from well-charged batteries for a month. We once went 22 days without an engine to replenish the batteries and still had plenty of reserve to radio the harbormaster in Antigua and let him know we were entering that crowded place under sail.

When you have determined that your alternator system is not functioning, there are three possible problems all amenable to correction at sea: belts, voltage regulators, and alternator replacement.

Belts. Most of the time the problem is either a broken or worn-out belt with which the engine turns the alternator. Replacement is a snap, unless your installation is so badly designed that other accessories must be removed to rebelt the alternator. If it is, you might consider hanging a spare belt inside the obstructing devices to be available for instant use.

Voltage Regulators. If an external regulator goes at sea and you do not have a replacement, take it out of the circuit and carefully monitor the recharging of your batteries for the rest of the passage. Monitoring means watching for little bubbles to start forming in the battery water. A boring job but it will get you home with healthy batteries. Anyway, most alternators have internal regulators these days.

Alternator Replacement. Replacing an alternator is dead easy. A couple of bolts, some electrical connections (be aware of the polarity!), a new belt, and off you go. If you are insecure about the project just watch any mechanic do it once before you leave. If you are enough of a minimal mechanic to check your oil, you can replace your alternator.

PAS DE BATTERIES

For as long as you sail you will be engaged in a never-ending dance to the death with your batteries. They have an aggravating internal chemistry capable of creating as many problems as you have solutions. The nicest thing to be said for batteries on a boat is that, although they die with expensive regularity, they die slowly, reluctantly, and generally one at a time. If you have two or more you will always have some battery power remaining at the end of the longest passage, that is if you had the good sense to reserve one out of the battery bank.

Keeping Batteries Alive. Here are some easy rules for keeping batteries alive:

The Easiest Rule: Keep them clean. Corroded terminals inhibit charging and drain power during use.

Another Easy Rule: Add water. Do not let the water level fall below a half-inch above the plates. When you are under heel for long periods, a proper water level is imperative.

A Fairly Easy Rule: Check specific gravity weekly. Your battery will die soon enough, so do not further shorten its life by letting it remain in a partially charged condition. Batteries should always be fully charged.

A Very Easy but Expensive Rule: Do not try to keep an ailing battery alive after reaching port. Replace it. You always want to start a passage with healthy batteries.

Electrical problems at sea do not require Thomas Alva Edison for their solution. Most are amenable to minimal mechanics. For the really unrepairable breakdowns you should have a backup. In the final analysis, you simply do not need all that galvanic fol-de-rol to get safely to port. Offshore passagemaking is electrifying enough and needs no generating system to give you a jolt that you will never forget.

Tracing and Stopping Water in the Bilge

Water will get into your boat. It can ooze into the tiniest openings, some of which you can see and some of which are invisible, or it can gush in if you let it. No boat I have ever known shipped no water at all.

THE BILGE WATER

There is always water in your bilge. You must learn to identify its nature and its source. It is vital that you differentiate between salt and sweet so that you can quickly trace a leak that manifests itself with an increase in bilge water. It takes a big hole to sink a boat, and if your boat is reasonably well designed, and if you have practiced getting to all parts of your bilge, you would have to have a violent confrontation with something big offshore to really threaten you.

The Automatic Bilge Pump. The chief danger is neither the sea nor holes in your boat. The chief danger is the ubiquitous, automatic, electric bilge pump. It has a Circean quality that first lulls you into thinking all is well and then hits you with an unpleasant surprise. You can go for months with the little nipper sucking at your bilge until you almost forget that it is there. One day, the nipper stops sucking and, since it has trained you not to bother with your bilge, your engine is suddenly awash and your batteries have salted out.

Checking the Bilge. It goes without saying that spare manual pumps should be carried, but they do not counter the bad habits created by the automatic power pumps. You should physically check your bilge twice a day. It is amazing what you will discover even if there is no water coming in.

Establishing a Salt Water Bilge "Norm." Depending on the point of sail and the water usage aboard, your boat will ship varying amounts of sea water. More in a beat than any other point of sail. In order to know when you are in trouble, it will be necessary to first determine how much water your boat normally takes on in each point of sail.

Sweet Water Leaks. Establish the normal intake for your boat, both sweet and salt, and be alert to any increase. Determine if any increase in the bilge is salt or sweet. Leaks into your bilge from your sweet water tanks can give an initial appearance of an intake of salt water through the hull. A slight water increase is no big deal as long as the water is salt. But any presence of sweet water, except after a significant rain, that will drain sweet down from the decks and into your bilge, can signal a disastrous loss of precious drinking water from your tanks, the last thing you want to happen on a long passage.

Two Sweet Water Danger Signals: When you develop a leak in your sweet water delivery system your waterpump will start "cycling" (turning on and off for short periods), thus alerting you that something funny is happening to your water supply. An evil-smelling bilge is also a sign that sweet water is accumulating. Salt water does not stink. Sweet water, like guests and fish, goes bad after a couple of days. Keep your ears alert for cycling and your nose alert for odors. These are the early warning signals of sweet water leaks, whether they originate from the water system or from the tanks themselves.

Intermittent Loss of Sweet Water: Sweet water leaks may mysteriously come and go. A tank may leak on a port tack and not to starboard, or may leak only in a rough sea. For this reason leaks oftimes only appear when you are already at sea. Just because your tanks do not leak when you are snugly tied to the dock is not a true indication of the condition of your tanks. Only extended sea trials will show up these and other faults.

Salt Water Leaks. "What if you spring a leak?" is the first thing landlubbers ask. It is very difficult to explain to nonsailors that, except in collisions, modern boats do not "spring" leaks. The term comes from the age of wooden boats when planks, bent to conform to the curves of the hull, would often "spring" free of their fastenings. Fiberglass does not spring. At worst it oozes.

Salt Water Oozes: Sea water naturally enters through the packing glands, by way of the port lights, through anchor hawse pipes, and insinuates itself into badly sealed joins. Some boats ooze more than others. You will soon learn the acceptable level for your particular boat. No sense trying to reduce the level at sea. When you get into port there will be plenty of time to fight the ooze. It is a battle that you will not win anyway.

Salt Water Gushes: A gush of sea water is always the result of a collision with a whale, another vessel, or a UFO (unidentified floating object). A gush will always be preceded by a loud bang. The sound of a small boat hitting anything in the water is magnified to apocalyptic proportions. When you hear a bang, any bang, dive for your bilge.

Getting at Salt Water Gushes: The only gush likely to sink you is one that you cannot get at. If you can reach the damage quickly you can always convert a gush to an ooze with almost any stuffing at hand. It is not possible to completely stop a leak. Sailors speak only of "stemming" leaks. But you need only stem it long enough to get to port. Stemming and pumping will keep you afloat. But first you must find the leak.

One of the problems with modern boats is that almost every inside surface is covered with something else. Surfaces contiguous to the water should be easy to expose. You do not want to start tearing bulkheads out at sea to repair a leak. Survey every internal surface for accessibility before you take off. If you have large areas that are not accessible, perhaps you should think of a little rebuilding.

Stemming a Salt Water Gush: Chances are that in any but a calmish sea you will not be able to get to the damage from *outside* the hull. Wind and water washing along the boat will prevent the attachment of patches. The only way to stem a leak is to stuff it from the inside. For stuffing just about anything at hand will do. Blankets, pillows, your lady's nighty, or your own jockey shorts. Just keep stuffing, don't think too much.

Après Stemming: If possible get your boat on a tack that keeps the damaged area out of the water. You should be able to limp a thousand miles on a dry tack, or at least until the seas and wind calm enough so you might be able to apply a patch from the outside.

As ever, we continue to preach that most crises at sea can be met and bested by amateurs such as you and me. You do not have to know too much in order to stuff a hole. That talent comes naturally. But do not lollygag.

CHAPTER **9**

Cultural Interface

VISAS AND PASSPORTS

Your small vessel has the same rights under maritime law as a supertanker or the QE2. Upon the presentation of the crew list and evidence of your ship's release from your last port, you have the theoretical and legal right to enter any port in the world in any ocean. You also have the right to enter any port "under protest" without documents of any kind.

There is no internationally accepted obligation directing you to obtain visas for yourself or your crew when you go abroad. Under maritime convention, a ship must be allowed entrance and, in most countries of the world, crew without visas are issued shore passes that allow them temporary access to the towns beyond the harbors.

You and your crew are neither tourists nor visitors. You have a special status as sailors, and while the host country, if it chooses, may infrequently prevent the crew from landing, it cannot prevent your vessel from entering. The host country has the right, however, to know who is coming ashore or, indeed, who remains on your vessel while in their harbor. Thus they have the right to request passports from all aboard whether or not they let them land.

While the host countries do not require visas, they will appreciate your courtesy in obtaining one. Most officials understand the yachtsman's special situation, but there is always the odd and cantankerous official who chooses to misunderstand and to give you a hard time. Should this contretemps arise, your best bet is to either turn around and sail out, or find someone to bribe. Chances are, at least in the Third World, that the "official difficulties" are being created for you with bribery in mind.

Passports represent a different sort of problem from visas. You are legally entitled to leave the U.S. without a passport. The problem is to find a carrier who will book your passage. If you are carrying yourself, in your own bottom, there is no problem in leaving, but without a passport at the other end of your journey you may not be allowed to land. Should you take unpassported crew aboard you may be obliged to keep them "forever," or at least until you can find a country that will accept them. In these days of national paranoia signing on unpassported folk is high folly to which you are well advised not to ascend. The reality these days is that passports have acquired the compelling cloak of legality. It has become difficult to move about the world without one. Get a passport. Incidentally, you may exit the U.S. without any document or any permission, but in order to return you must have proof of citizenship. A passport is nice in these circumstances but a simple U.S. birth certificate will do very well.

One last note concerning passports. Should you lose yours, or have it lifted (more likely), any U.S. Consulate or Embassy will issue a new one in just a few hours. You will have to establish some evidence of citizenship such as a voter registration card, a birth certificate, your social security card, a driver's license or, when all else fails, the names of four NFL quarterbacks. In any event, report the loss of your passport *immediately*, lest you later discover, upon returning home, that an alter ego bearing your identity is wandering about the landscape.

Visa Requirements of Foreign Governments

Every country has its own special set of requirements for obtaining a visa. Requirements vary widely and some countries demand the most precise entry and exit information while some require no visa at all. It is easier to get a visa from the foreign consular representative located in your own country than to try to get one abroad. For sailors, a visa and close date requirements involve special difficulties since the schedule of a small sailing vessel is at best loose and mostly nonexistent. So get your visas if you must, ahead of time. Even though you may miss the dates, the possession of a visa granted in your own country will make it easier while abroad to get a new one or an extension.

Visas cannot be procured in a country in which you have already arrived. Should you plan on applying when you arrive, you will find yourself turned around and shipped out. I once flew into Japan with an expired visa and found myself in Korea the next day applying for a visa to Japan.

Check with the State Department for the requirements of the countries you wish to visit.

ADJUSTMENTS AND EXPECTATIONS

When you sail away from the shores of the U.S. you leave behind a set of rules to which you have become accustomed in your life. These agreements are the social contract that you have made with your fellow Americans, the concord to which all must subscribe. They include the laws to which you have agreed to abide and the rules of conduct that most of us follow.

We know what is legally required of us for the laws are written down. We have learned by growing up in our society what the culturally dictated limits of proper conduct and good taste are. We all know how we are supposed to act toward our government and toward each other.

When you sail into a foreign port you will begin to realize the enormous gulf that separates a rich and blessed U.S. from almost all of the rest of the world. Your hosts live in a different world than yours and have different expectations about how you should act. You are an irritant, coming into their settled world like a stone tossed into a glassy millpond. Your mere presence makes waves. Do not, through lack of understanding of your hosts, magnify those waves into a tempest. If you do it will be at your expense. It is after all their country.

A mismatch of cultural expectations can be uncomfortable and expensive. For example, bargaining is expected in most of the Third World, and the buyer who pays the initial price asked is thought a fool. In Red China one never makes advances toward a female comrade but, on the other hand, close across the sea in Taiwan, another Chinese society, women are often considered the silver by which deals are signed. In Japan the failure to return a gift (which gift is then returned with another and another and another) is considered the worst of taste. For societies as similar as ours, to the English the phrase "knocked up" (awakened in the morning) is acceptable but the word "bloody" is not. The list of confronts is endless, so make no assumptions that foreigners do things the way you do them at home. The best advice is to carefully observe and imitate what goes on about you.

BONA FIDE

You never know which piece of paper will satisfy which foreign official. Most foreign folk stand in awe of the printed form *cum* signature and will prostrate themselves before any document sealed with wax. A good idea is to affix U.S. stamps to any document you carry and go to your friendly local post office to cancel them. The stamp means "official," the one thing with which most folk in the Third World do not want to fool around.

Document yourself to the hilt. Include the following and be creative in extending the list.

Passport, of course. A passport is yours by right and can only be denied if you have been really naughty, and there is even a question about that.

Birth Certificate. Obtainable from the office of the municipal registration clerk of the town in which you were born.

Voter Registration Card. The municipality in which you claim residence will issue this identification.

Amateur Radio License. Obtainable from the Federal Communication Commission upon passing a proficiency test. Tests are scheduled throughout the U.S. Ask at any ham radio store to put you in touch with the local ham club. (Look it up in the yellow pages.) They are everywhere and are passionate proselytizers committed to helping you get your ham license.

Permit to Purchase Guns. This is a permit to purchase to which you are entitled and not a permit to carry a concealed weapon, which is a special and difficult right to obtain. A U.S. permit to purchase guns will suffice as a license to own abusive firepower in most of the wilder parts of the world. Do not go abroad without a permit, whether you plan to carry weapons or not.

Store Receipts for Guns and Ammo. Always useful for cranky officials.

International Driver's License. Can be obtained from almost any travel agency. If you want to rent a car abroad this is most useful.

Honorary Deputy Sheriff's Badge. Meaningless at home but impressive abroad.

Letters of Introduction from: your governor, your mayor, your congressman, any politician with a fancy title and good stationery, your yacht club, your chief of police (very important), and the "American Association of Practically Anything." (Are you beginning to get the idea?)

The more stuff you have the more authentic you appear. If you have enough pieces of paper, one of them will be exactly what someone is looking for. A good idea is to form, by the simple act of printing stationery, the "American Association for the Study of Blue Water Oil Pollution," or suchlike title. Write yourself a letter on AASBWOP stationery authorizing yourself to make a research study of the deep oceans. For good measure add a rubber stamp to the signature. Works like a charm!

THE PRICE OF ADMISSION

One of the most perseverant tales among sailorly folk concerns the arrogance and the intransigence of foreign officialdom. I have not found this particular piece of mythology to be true. I have found most officials, even when venal and grasping, to be reasonably easy to get along with, so long as you take the trouble to see the problems you represent through their eyes. As soon as you make this perceptual leap, the whole confusing and aggravating matter of entrance documentation becomes reasonable and understandable.

Crew List

Crew lists are required so that your hosts can know that they are only extending hospitality to someone they *want* in their country. Also, the host country has the right to be sure that you are departing with all the folk you brought in, and are not leaving anyone lying about. If there were no crew lists, the smuggling of illegals would be a simple and unstoppable business.

The crew list is usually required in anywhere from three to six copies, and must be attested to and signed by the skipper. In order to deal easily with this crucial entrance document, have copies made at the start of the voyage. When preparing crew lists ahead of time, throw everything in. Officials like lots of printed stuff to play with:

Name, middle name, first name

Place and date of birth

Father's name

Mother's name

Citizen of what country

Passport number and where issued

Social Security number

With these seven pieces of information, you should be able to carry your crew into any country in the world, especially if they bear a very official looking seal of the vessel. (A rubber stamp or, better yet, an embossing device. Get one.)

Release from the Previous Port (Port Clearance)

No host country wants to give shelter to a boat already in trouble in another port. The release informs your new host that you obeyed the laws of your previous host, and that you did not try to sneak out without paying the victualer and the oiler. Look upon it as a letter of introduction attesting to your good character.

Stores List

Stores lists are meant to provide the host country with the assurance that the boat's stores, food and suchlike, will not be illegally smuggled ashore. With a stores list the host can physically check what supplies were aboard at entering, and what may reasonably be expected to be aboard at departure. They can, but they rarely do.

The stores list usually has a section labeled cargo. Always answer "none" to this query. You are not a cargo vessel, and should you give the impression that you are, all sorts of bad, confusing, and expensive things will happen to you.

To every host, the crucial matters on the stores list are alcohol, tobacco, guns, and ammunition. Be *very* careful of these, most especially in Third World countries. Alcohol in the Arab world is a no-no, and tobacco has always been the international means of black-market exchange. List exactly what you have aboard. *No one will be upset at what you have, only at what you fail to declare.* Things can get very sticky if your host gets the notion that you are purposely trying to hide something.

Prepare a careful inventory of guns and each and every round of ammunition. Many hosts will count the shells when you arrive and before you depart to make sure that you have not fired off a few or sold them to the local insurgency. List guns by make, model, type, and caliber, and list ammunition by caliber. Most hosts do not mind your having guns on board, just so long as they can assure themselves that you take out with you exactly what you brought in and that you have not used them while you were in their waters. The stores list accomplishes this.

Provide a lockable cabinet, called bond locker, in the boat that the officials can seal. It is much better than having your weapons taken off the boat for safekeeping. Sometimes you will not get them back, and it is always an awful hassle. Under no circumstances must you allow the official seal on your arms locker to be broken while you are in port. You are on your honor and they mean it.

In this day and age of liberating electronics, there are many countries who consider a fax machine or a copier to be more dangerous than an assault rifle. Officials will always want to know how many of these potentially "revolutionary" devices you have aboard, and will take great pains to make sure they go out with you.

We entered Shanghai in 1982, the first western sailboat to do so since World War II. We were there at the invitation of the Government, to help teach the mainland Chinese to build fiberglass boats which were, at the time, providing so much hard currency to the Taiwanese.

There were a number of confrontations with officialdom so totally inexperienced in dealing with a privately owned sailboat. The first difficulty surfaced with the matter of a pilot required to get up the Yangtse and on into the Wang Poo. The Chinese put a pilot aboard who, unused to a sailboat's motion, became violently seasick and remained so till we tied to the dock which had been specially built for us.

When we received the pilotage bill it was for $6000. We complained and were told that their Coast Guard only had one regulation for piloting big boats up the Yangtse and nowhere did it stand written that little sailboats were any different. We were being charged the same fee that applied to the great merchant ships that entered Shanghai. We protested for two years until both they and we tired of arguing.

As we tied up we were boarded, as is usual, by medical, military, immigration and other folk all fascinated by our private yacht . . . the first they had ever seen. When the police started their look-see, we asked what we were to do with the guns we carried. To our surprise, they seemed puzzled by the question and indicated that there was no problem with our having weapons. We were even more surprised when we asked, nervously, about much of what we felt might be considered "counter-revolutionary" books and publications that we carried.

The police brushed our concerns about writings aside and then, in the course of looking through our galley, the search took a very serious turn and the searchers grew most stern.

"What," we asked, "seems to be the problem?"

"There is a very serious violation aboard your boat," the chief police officer replied, "and you will be required to either lock up the material that concerns us or leave at once."

"Of course, of course, we will be happy to comply," we answered, totally puzzled by what aboard, if not guns or ideas, so upset our Chinese hosts.

"You must immediately," the officer said, "at once and for as long as you are with us," and here he paused and lowered his voice to a conspiratorial whisper lest onlookers overhear him, "lock up your food!"

There we had it. Guns and ideas did not violate the Chinese revolutionary spirit, but all that panoply of rich food we carried was judged to be subversive. Talk about cultural conflicts.

Deratting Certificate

The easiest entry document to get is a deratting certificate or a deratting exemption. This document is designed for big ships on which rats are a problem. But if you want the privileges of the big boats then you must accept their obligations. Get the paperwork done as soon as you can. It means very little, but cranky officials could make it into a federal case should they choose, as they once did with me in Indonesia.

Immunization Certificate

Before you leave the U.S. get yellow international immunization certificates for every member of your crew. They only become important should you have the bad luck to be in a part of the world in which an epidemic has flared up. No one pays much attention to the expiration dates, and forms are rarely asked for, but they are invaluable when needed.

That is all you need to get into any port in the world. The important thing is to be respectful, quietly follow the rules, and dutifully fill in all the proffered paperwork. And never, never lie about your weapons.

UNIVERSAL ENTRANCE DOCUMENT

The document on page 201 is one I use in every port I enter. In designing a form for your own passages there may be categories of information I have overlooked. Add them as you please, and add stamps or seals. The larger and the more official looking the document, the more it will be respected.

THIS WAY TO THE EGRESS

It's a bit more difficult to get out of a country than it is to get in. When you come in you are under a quarantine flag and the officials must come to you since you are not allowed off the boat. When you want to leave you must go find them and that is sometimes not so easy. Allow yourself an entire day and be pleasantly surprised if it requires only half that time.

Before you leave you must satisfy the police, immigration, customs, and the captain of the port. The police wants to check your weapons locker and make sure that you have behaved. Immigration wants to be sure that your crew is the same as your previously filed crew list. If there are any changes to the crew you will need documentation from immigration of proper entry, or exit papers for crew who are either leaving or joining your vessel. Customs wants to be sure that you are not smuggling out anything improper (an antiquity, a piece of coral, currency of the country), and the captain of the port will give you clearance to your next port if he has had no complaints from merchants that you owe money. Do not get into a hassle with the local merchants. They always turn out to be the brother-in-law of the captain of the port.

Be polite, be firm, be fair, and give in to reasonable demands even if they are unreasonable. It is, after all, their country.

BRIBERY AND BAKSHEESH

Everybody, absolutely everybody, does it. But it must be done correctly lest you cause an official to lose face or, heaven forfend, you offer to grease a lesser man and his superior finds out. For your first lessons in the native attitude toward bribery, go immediately to the other yachts that arrived before you. They will have gleaned from their predecessors, who learned in turn from their predecessors, how the locals like things to be done.

It must be precisely understood that bribery abroad is always offered for legal things to which you are entitled. It is a method of getting things done, a sliding around the law within acceptable limits. It is never explicitly offered to break a law, and it is never, never offered if you are caught in *flagrante delicto*. If you are apprehended in an illegal act, offering to bribe the police will often be accepted but will seldom help and is as likely as not to compound your difficulties.

Should you actually get arrested and put in the pokey, you belong to the judge. And that is a different, delicate, and much, much, more expensive matter.

ENTRANCE DOCUMENT

United States Sailing Vessel

UNLIKELY VII

PARTICULARS

SAILBOAT: Cutter Rig | **LENGTH:** 46 Feet | **GROSS TONNAGE:**

SAILS: Red | **BEAM:** 13 Feet | 22 Tons

HULL: White | **DRAFT:** 6 Feet | **NET TONNAGE:** 17

REGISTRATION
U.S.A. Documentation: Number 618721
Hailing Port: Atlantic City, NJ, U.S.A.
Master's License: Sailing Vessels Less
than 100 Tons
Amateur Radio Call Sign: KA2AUP

STORES (no cargo)   Tobacco   Alcohol

ARMS Ithaca Shotgun #371600609
Smith & Wesson 38 #D599802

AMMUNITION 12-Gauge Shotgun Shells (262)
38 Caliber Rounds (606)

CREW LIST (No Passengers Aboard)

NAME   CITIZEN OF   PASSPORT NUMBER

_____

_____

LAST PORT_____ DATE DEPARTED _____
NEXT PORT_____ DEPARTURE DATE _____

(SEAL)

_____   _____
Signature and seal   *Date*

Whom to Bribe

Officialdom in most of the dingier ports of the world buy their posts and receive a totally insufficient salary. The purchase of an office that pays practically nothing is really the purchase of a quasi-official franchise to extract bribes.

The high officials get very testy if you try to bribe their inferiors. Bribe money is meant to float down, it never quite gets to float up. Should you start bribing at too low a level, the most entitled official with the most power is deprived and becomes angered, unfortunately not at his inferiors, but at you since it was you who cut him out of the action.

The best advice is to bribe the very highest official who will accept a bribe. If an official will not, it generally means that you have climbed too high on the baksheesh ladder and have missed a designated and trusted junior bagman who has been given the honor of actually accepting the cash. So keep climbing until you reach closed doors, then back down one rung and reach for your wallet, confident that everybody will get theirs and no one will be mad at you.

How to Bribe

Every country will have its own little charade concerning the actual offering. No one will turn down a bribe but often you will get a show of dismay and resistance. Press on, this is only face-saving. The offer will be accepted in the end. It is, however, never proper to offer a bribe in front of the bribee's inferiors and you must never, never discuss with the foot soldiers how much your bribe to the general was. Conventionally the "big guy" will later share the bribe with his inferiors and, since he certainly may want to cheat a bit, it is better that only he knows how much you gave him.

How Much to Bribe

It might be that a gift of cheap jewelry or a bottle of liquor will do the deal. But ultimately all will want cash, real spendable stuff, preferably dollars that they can change on the black market. Westerners always bribe and tip too much. We are not loved for it, indeed, we are thought fools and easy marks for other scams. Start with the offer of a pittance, an amount so small that, should you have miraculously stumbled onto that rare un-bribeable official, it will appear as a small joke between friends and not a bribe at all. Most officials will quietly decline the initial offerings and wait expectantly. Keep upping the offer, displaying increasing dismay at the fortune he is extracting from you. Unless you can convince him that it hurts, he will continue to wait. But he will stop and take the money long before you become really outraged. Foreign officials have exquisite noses for how much can be extracted.

We were holed up in Hurghada on the Egyptian coast of the Red Sea. We had ducked in after losing our engine.

The assistant Captain of the Port, Achmed, short, fat and wheezy had eyes on everything aboard. Like an experienced schnorrer he started his depredations modestly . . . a pack of cigarettes, a can of soup, some soap, and not too gradually escalated his demands to include serious stuff like radios and diving equipment.

Not wanting to cause him to invent problems for us we sought out his weaknesses of which the main was women. We had made many not so sly references to the ladies that we had aboard and in a moment of painful truthfulness he confessed that his successes were less than he would hope for.

We smelled a bureaucratic sexist rat. Encouraged by our interest he let slip that he was having some difficulty "running his flag up" and it was causing him great embarrassment not only with the ladies with whom he should not be dallying, but, more importantly for his middle eastern macho image of self, with his very own wife.

Had we, he whispered one day, ever heard of such a condition?

We confessed that we had.

Being American and having such wonderful American medicines, did we . . . ?

We cut him off with instant assurance that the wonderful American medical world from which we came had exactly the correct remedy for his condition. Even more wonderful, we confided, we had the exact remedy aboard. Could he come back the next day to get it—you bet he could!

That evening we carefully removed the labels from a jar of innocent moisturizing cream and lettered in official looking style the legend *American Sex Cream.*

We gave it to the poor fellow the next day with instructions for its use and asked that he report its effectiveness. Achmed went off clutching the jar of American Sex Cream. If it could help him, he told us, he would be our man in all troublesome matters.

Achmed showed up the next morning wreathed in smiles and contentment, his image of manhood restored.

"American medicine is truly as wonderful as we are told," he chortled, "now, my friends, in what ways can I be of assistance to you?"

We counted the ways and for the rest of our stay in Hurghada, at the cost of a jar of cosmetic cream, we could do no wrong.

CASH AND CARRYING

An assortment of currencies is the best. The denizens of every country you will visit have their own preferences and prejudices concerning the kind of cash they like to receive. In most of the

Third World if you are American they will want greenbacks. Since no currency regulation limits your right to carry your own currency, and since endless regulations concern what you may and may not do with theirs, the best money to carry is U.S. dollars.

The best dollar bill is the hundred dollar bill. Foreigners all over the world know the look and the feel of a hundred and, because of familiarity, are more willing to accept it than a ten or a twenty. I found that the "high caste" black money dealers in India, from whom the best rates could be had, would deal only in hundreds. Anything smaller was considered *déclassé*. The other reason for the popularity of a hundred dollars is that most of the U.S. cash passed abroad is smuggled out of the host country by those to whom you are paying it. Hundreds make a small, smuggleable, easily disguised package.

Dangers of the Black Market

A word of caution about black, gray, and otherwise off-color street markets. Although black markets are ubiquitous, they are universally illegal. You have no recourse when cheated. And while there are ways to avoid being cheated, the chances are that the money changers are a damn-site slyer than you are.

While the black market is tricky, it is also irresistible. When you are offered 20 to 30 percent more on the black market than in the banks, as you will in most parts of the Third World, it is very hard to toss away the advantage. If you are really nervous, the American on the next boat who has been in port for a long time will offer you almost as good a deal in your own cabin as you would get in the alley. The safest way, and in my book the only way, to change money on the black market is through a friend who is a citizen of your host country. He will have had long experience with the money changers and will always know a dealer who values his repeated custom. Dealers in money, like more ordinary retailers, will rarely rook a regular. So find a local friend to be your banker.

On Hiding Money

Since dollars are deliciously negotiable, they must be cleverly squirreled away aboard your boat. Theft of money from boats is a continuing reality. Thieves can be your own crew, occasional visitors to your boat, professionals who make their living off yachties, or the police or other corrupt officials. The sequestering of cash must be a highly secret operation.

Never hide all your bills in one place. Use a number of sanctuaries so that if a thief diminishes your cash, he will not destroy your ability to continue your passage. Do not put bills in books or behind hollow panels. Those are the first places to be searched. Do not hide a safe in a bulkhead. You will not only lose its contents, but much damage will occur as it is torn out.

Nowhere in this book do I advise that you take the slightest chance of breaking any foreign laws. Even when you exchange money on the black market let someone else take the risk. I am law abiding and if you are going passaging so should you be. However there is this one exception, and in this exception you must *never* obey the law. On entering most foreign countries you will be asked to write down the amount of cash you are carrying and in which currencies.

My advice to you is to lie. If you are carrying a lot of cash, especially in the Third World, and it becomes known in official circles, some hungry customs officer, or even perhaps the big chief of the port himself, will peddle that valuable information to the local mafia. In this case, while obeying the law, you are prone to get banged on the head. Declaration of large amounts of cash is an invitation to surreptitious intrusion. Instead of being truthful, estimate what you feel would be a proper and modest sum to be carrying, cut it in half, and declare it in Indian rupees. Nobody wants Indian rupees.

The Insatiable Greed for Gold

The next best way, maybe even the best way, to carry money is in the form of gold. Gold has been around for a long time and is a means of exchange underestimated by none (except perhaps the ancient Incas who made a bad bargain with the Spaniards). Aborigines and arbitrageurs alike will lean toward gold like a morning glory leans into the sun. In places where no medium has much value, where even greenbacks are discounted, and where American Express cards are scorned, a heavy purse of gold can do the deal.

Until recently, the Krugerrand was widely known and accepted. However, the Krugerrand, while no less valued, is becoming less preferred than the more obscure Canadian maple leaf coinage. The all-time best will be the golden eagles that the U.S. Treasury is proposing to mint. If they appear, they will be the true sailor's shekel.

Gold must be hidden no less cleverly than paper money, but since it is heavy, disguising gold is a bit more difficult. There is one nifty place aboard any sailboat where gold can be hidden, and can be found neither by accident nor design. Here is my secret. Do not tell anybody.

At the bottom of your gimballed stove, under the oven, there is a sealed compartment enclosing some metal weights used to damp the swing of the stove in a heavy sea. Conceal your gold in that compartment. It will help the damping process, confound sneak thieves, and should you ever be faced with the prospect of a search by venal officials, as I have, just turn on the oven and bake something. Nobody wants to fool around with a hot stove.

Passaging on Plastic

In many countries you can now use your VISA/MasterCard, issued by an American bank, to draw cash locally in the foreign currency.

The plastic disease, already pandemic in the U.S., is quickly spreading throughout the rest of the world. I have passed VISA in China, AmEx in the Maldives, Diners in Oman, and in Bombay I never lacked for a Lac of Rupees. Only in Port Sudan was nothing accepted save U.S. hundreds and gold. But, then again, there was nothing to buy except elephant hair bracelets, of which you can quickly acquire too many.

The Platinum Card, issued by American Express, costs you a fee each year just for the privilege of carrying it. It is worth it. It is the ultimate open sesame. A flash of the Platinum makes headwaiters cringe, tables appear by legerdemain, hotel rooms are magically built in a twinkling where none existed before, and should you be so inclined, the Platinum is better than a gypsy violinist and a dozen roses in a *passage d'amour*.

WORKING YOUR WAY

Saleable and Nonsaleable Skills

Paradoxically, the only folk for whom there is no market outside the U.S. are lawyers and bankers. Almost any other skill or profession will find a market. The obvious ones are construction skills such as carpentry, plumbing, and electrical. All over the world, and especially in the Third World, there is always a call for folk to carry forward construction projects. Even if you are not the most proficiently skilled worker, chances are that you have far more technical smarts and more experience than your hosts.

Work Permits

One of the problems of working ashore is that most countries require work permits and in some places they are difficult to get. The reality is that, the more difficult permits are to get, the more easily local contractors get around the need for them. Find a job and let your boss get you the permit. If he needs you there will be no problem.

The most difficult country in which to get a work permit is probably Japan, and yet there are thousands of Westerners, none of whom have work permits, few of whom have any training, and all of whom earn a good living tutoring English. But what is safe in Japan could be very dangerous in the Third World. Make sure that you get your employer to do the necessary or, at least, to be responsible in the event there is a brouhaha.

Selling to Other Sailors: No Permits Required

Sailors can and do much of their own work but almost all need specialized services. Rigging repair and tuning, hull repair, and sail repair are the most obvious fields. A knowledge of diesel engines, and the tools for basic repair, maintenance, and overhaul, are always in demand. Anyone with an oscilloscope, a working knowledge of electronics, and the repair manuals of electronic instruments will do very well indeed. I know of no boat that does not have *some* electronic problem.

No sailboat is free of storage battery and alternator problems. The day that electrical systems are installed on boats is the same day that they begin to seriously fail, and since most marine installation represents shoddy work, the rate of failure is breathtaking. If you have the skills, it would not be difficult or expensive to mount a first-rate electrical repair facility on even a small sailboat. The rebuilding of alternators alone could keep you afloat.

The Almighty (Well Almost) Pen

Writing about the sea is no easy job. It pays little, is terribly competitive, the income is discontinuous, and the rejection slips emotionally deep-six you into funk. In spite of all this, many of us write even though few of us are chosen. Most writers do so because they cannot not do so. We are inwardly compelled to share our thoughts and ideas, and we write even though we are aware that publication is hard and payment is almost nonexistent.

If you are lucky enough to get a book published, or to have a few magazine articles a year accepted, you may be able to deduct most or all of your travel and boat costs as tax-deductible expenses (ask your accountant). Uncle Sam recognizes, albeit reluctantly, that folk who get paid to write about the sea must perforce be at sea to do so. A boat is as necessary to a sailor/author as an office is to a businessman. Escaping to sea from the demands and the drudgeries of the land is the reason that most of us are out there. Escaping from income taxes can be an unexpectedly delicious icing on the sweet cake of passagemaking.

Crew Who Pay Their Way

Passage expenses can often be recouped by taking along crew who will contribute to the operational costs of the boat. Paying crew can be a pain in the butt since you have chosen them for their ability to pay rather than for the sweetness of their personalities. Unless you are extraordinarily lucky, or have the gentle soul of Aquinas, this sort of crew will end up demanding more than they are worth and more than you are willing to give. Remember, also, the danger of contravening the terms of your insurance policy. Many policies forbid the carrying of passengers and paying crew are, to say the least, in a gray legal area.

If you do risk this method of financing your passages, do not sign on people for long periods of time. Agree only to take them to the next port. By that time, chances are you will both want to see each others' backs. If not, and if they turn out to be really nifty, you can always take them along for another leg. But only one leg at a time.

The Chartering Option

If your insurance policy and the laws of your host country allow it, short-term chartering is a possible source of income. Possible but not easy, since charter guests make heavy demands on the boat and the crew. They demand a much higher level of comfort and convenience than you are equipped for, and the cost of laying in all that extra stuff can cut into your earnings. They always want to go when you want to stay and they always want to go to places that you know are lousy. The local laws can be a big hurdle even if there is a big demand for charter boats, and as soon as the locals see that you are earning good money they either start generating governmental interference or demanding baksheesh.

If you love your boat, chartering her is much like renting out your wife and hanging about to supervise the activities. Never a satisfactory arrangement. Better you should work for a living.

Don't Wait to Go Offshore

I again urge you to go offshore, to strange and foreign lands, for great chunks of time, long before you are rich enough to retire. If you wait until you have enough security, a heavy safe could fall on your head and you may never get to go at all. When you go on an offshore passage it is unlikely that you will be reduced to penury; the worst scenario is that you will discover strengths and weaknesses about yourself that the cotton wool padding of your present life will never allow you to learn.

Get out there. Put yourself in harm's way. Discover just who that wonderfully unique adventurer inside of you really is. Accept risk till you come to know that risk accepted is risk defeated. Find the warm and comforting inner security that comes from having dared and done what the rest of the world only dreams about. Go. Now!

End Log

To those of you who have furrowed their way through this book, I offer a word of caution and a word of praise.

The praise is in recognition that this has not been an easy, predigested, and organized book. The act of making sailors out of sow's ears quickly, so that you do not waste your best years— any year is a best year—trundling about the land, requires a large dollop of higgledy-piggledyness. Indeed a sailor is never really finished like a piece of toast or a steak. A sailor is always in the living process of becoming, a condition described by Plato as life itself.

There is too damned much information, too much experience, and too many variables for any sailor to absorb in one lifetime. You are a sailor when you say you are a sailor, not when you know this much or that much. That is the core of this book. To give enough information, but just enough, to support a claim to sailordom, and to convince you that, with the minimums set up herein, you are capable of taking a small boat across a large ocean.

From the first page this book has dumped onto your head, helter skelter, undigested impedimenta of ocean sailing. Facts, techniques, and theories, mostly unranked in importance, cascade down and pile up around you. This is no cogent, thoughtful, how-to book. It is only the opening salvo, the beginning process that will stretch out, in joy and delight, for the rest of your life.

Learning takes place by impact, by jamming in information till the mind, seemingly of its own free will, makes some sense of it all. Real learning is revelation, almost mystical, almost religious, and real learning about the sea comes to us only in that mode. Should you wait for that moment of revelation before going to sea you will waste too much precious life. We must go to sea before we are replete with perfect knowledge. We must go to sea slightly confused, not even knowing what we know, and let the sea put things together for us. We must load ourselves and the facts, the minimum facts, onto a sailboat and set out. Understanding of the sea will only happen at sea to those who have gathered together the basic grab bag of information. That is what this book is, a grab bag of tools and ideas that your hands-on experience, far at sea, will fashion into sailorly wisdom.

Do not wait on the land for wisdom to occur. Set to sea where life is.

> *Goodbye to things that bore me.*
> *Life is waiting for me.*
> *I see a new horizon, my life has only begun.*
> *Beyond the blue horizon lies a rising sun.*

BOSTON PUBLIC LIBRARY

3 9999 03140 402 1

VANGUE

Gaga

I.S. Thomæ

DAMUTE
hic effoditur aurum
in magna copia

MANI
CON
GO.

OCEANI

Angola

AFRIC AE

CAFATES

GAVI

ZET

PA R S

GOIRS

AETHIOPICI

P A R S

MAITAG ASI

MONO

ZEFA LA

MOTA
BUTUA

PA

Delineatio orarum Manicongi, Angolæ,
Monomotapæ, terræ natalis Zofalæ, Mozambicæ Abyssinorum & una cum vadis, et furtibus adjacentibus. Item insula magna vulgo
S. Laurentij alias Madagascar dictæ, inter
maximas totius Orientis habitæ.